D1282001

AUTOBIOGRAPHY
OF A
SADHU

"An authentic and fascinating account of a Western yogi who has made India his home for his body and his spirit. *Autobiography of a Sadhu* is bound to challenge your view of reality and the spiritual life. It is not just the story of a personal quest but of a journey beyond the Western civilization mind-set to the real India of the yogis, where the limitations of both our cultural ideas and our egos are continually exposed. An adventure into a different kind of reality."

DAVID FRAWLEY, DIRECTOR OF THE
AMERICAN INSTITUTE OF VEDIC STUDIES
AND AUTHOR OF *YOGI AND AYURVEDA*
AND *YOGA AND THE SACRED FIRE*

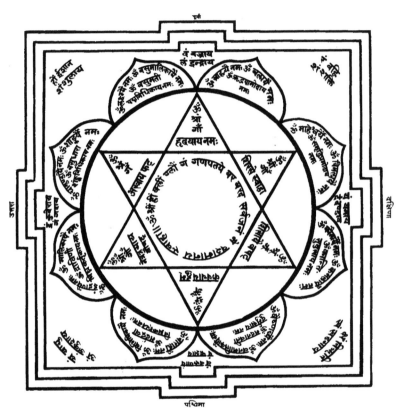

A Lakshmi Ganesh yantra, bestowing proposerity and success.

AUTOBIOGRAPHY OF A SADHU

A Journey into Mystic India

RAMPURI

Destiny Books

Rochester, Vermont • Toronto, Canada

Destiny Books
One Park Street
Rochester, Vermont 05767
www.DestinyBooks.com

Destiny Books is a division of Inner Traditions International

Copyright © 2005, 2010 by Baba Rampuri

Originally published in 2005 by Bell Tower, New York, under the title *BABA: Autobiography of a Blue-Eyed Sadhu*

All rights reserved. No part of this book may be reproduced or utilized in any form or by any means, electronic or mechanical, including photocopying, recording, or by any information storage and retrieval system, without permission in writing from the publisher.

Library of Congress Cataloging-in-Publication Data
Rampuri.
 [Baba]
 Autobiography of a sadhu : a journey into mystic India / Rampuri.
  p. cm.
 "Originally published in 2005 by Bell Tower, New York, under the title Baba : autobiography of a blue-eyed sadhu."
 ISBN 978-1-59477-330-3 (pbk.)
 1. Rampuri. 2. Yogis—India—Biography. 3. Yogis—United States—Biography.
I. Title.
 BL1175.R34295A3 2010
 294.5'092—dc22
 [B]

                                                                    2009045708

Printed and bound in Lake Book Manufacturing

10 9 8 7 6 5 4 3 2 1

Text design by Jon Desaultels
Text layout by Virginia Scott Bowman
This book was typeset in Garamond Premier Pro with Papyrus as the display typeface

Contents

Acknowledgments

I would like to thank the following people for making this Destiny Books edition possible: Dieter Hagenbach, Sigi Hoehle, Adriana Knezevic, Ehud Sperling, Ossi Urchs, and Bikram Choudhury.

It is only by the Grace of God
That one yearns for Union with Him,
And escapes serious danger.

THE AVADHUT GITA OF DATTATREYA

Introduction

I was born on the fourteenth of July, celebrated in France as the day of the emancipation of prisoners from the infamous Bastille prison and the beginning of the French Revolution. And, although I have traveled to the edges of the world of my birth, my journey began in the middle of things: I arrived in the middle of the day, the month, the year, and the century, as well as in the middle of the American continent, Chicago, where my father was then a surgeon. But the future for my family lay in sunny California, where my father would be able to realize the American Dream; so we moved to Beverly Hills in 1953, and, with one loan from his father-in-law, and another from the bank, he bought a brand-new Studebaker.

My first spiritual initiation took place at the age of four. Televisions were relatively new then and looked like half-size wood-paneled refrigerators with small screens. Inspired by *The Adventures of Superman* and wearing a large red bandana around my neck, I climbed to the top of the television as if ascending Mount Sinai, and made a great leap into space, as my hero would have done. My flight was obviously doomed, but something happened when I crashed to the floor that changed my life forever. I saw stars inside my head.

"What are you, stupid? That's what happens when you hit your

1

head," said my father impatiently, as he drove me to his office to get stitches. "Why on earth would such a smart boy like you do such a silly thing?" asked my mother.

I knew that there was no use telling her about the clanging bells. There are certain things you just have to keep to yourself. You can't explain them to people incapable of understanding them. I had seen the same stars inside my head as I saw in the sky on the rare clear night, and I wanted to know how they had gotten in there.

But what I was really into was buried treasure. I dug up the whole of the backyard looking for some but never found anything. Messing up the earth is one thing, but damaging property is another matter, so, when convinced that a treasure must be there, I hacked a huge hole in the garage roof with my father's favorite golf club, I faced the belt.

"There are no buried treasures," my father told me. "There is only hard work and the money you receive for it, and that's the reality of life." I didn't believe him. *There's got to be more,* I thought.

I imagined my grandfather, who left Russia when he was thirteen, to be Long John Silver, the infamous pirate. After all, he had crossed the Atlantic Ocean three times: once to explore the world and discover America, next to bring his family to the "promised land," and a third time when he spirited his true love, my grandmother, through Europe to Mexico and then to her new home in Corpus Christi, Texas. I would sit for hours listening to his stories of adventure in foreign lands: the people, customs, and languages, and his tales of survival not by money but by wits. He told me of desperate situations, how he pulled through, and the lessons he learned that I was now learning. One day he gave me a small treasure, a silver dollar, a modern "piece of eight."*

---

*A Spanish doubloon (gold coin) spoken of in all the pirate adventure stories, most notably in Robert Louis Stevenson's *Kidnapped,* whose memorable character was Long John Silver, mentioned above.

Treasures are buried so that they can be found again, I thought, and hid my silver coin in the backyard, carefully drawing a map of where I had put it. I never did find it again. It didn't seem to be where I had buried it—or was my map inaccurate? When I gave up my search, I swore that when I grew up, I would unearth a real treasure.

At about the time my self-identity—that of a cowboy-pirate—began to crystallize, the hard reality of school threatened its very existence. I had to learn to be someone else, in fact, two people—one for those in authority and one for peers. My goals of secret knowledge, magic, and buried treasure would have to be hidden from all authority for fear of punishment, and from peers for fear of ridicule. From there, I went on to be a model student, athlete, and citizen until the mid-sixties.

My mother wanted me to become president of the United States, but suspected I might become a dictator, so she settled for a wealthy lawyer. My father wanted me to become a doctor, but his hopes were dashed when, the first time I accompanied him and scrubbed up to observe him perform a minor surgery, I fainted at the sight of blood.

As the sixties progressed and we went from one Kennedy assassination to another, to the murder of Martin Luther King Jr., and from race riots to the Vietnam War, I found myself with few answers to my many questions and doubts, and fewer places to turn to. I was becoming an outsider, an unbeliever. I found it increasingly difficult to live in the comfortable, insulated world of the bourgeois. Instead of thanking God for the privilege of affluence, I questioned it. I could no longer accept what I saw and touched as reality; it was paper-thin, and I could see through it. My mind was tender then, and I began to glimpse the chaos beneath the surface, beneath all the niceties and order.

At that same time I discovered that I was not who I thought I was, and neither was I who everyone else supposed me to be. The real guy was in there somewhere, buried among a mound of temporary identities, and I needed to find a way back to myself.

I felt so much smallness in my very big world. Beverly Hills with its eternal promise of fabulous wealth, fame, and glitter was just too small. I wanted something so big that it wouldn't fit on a television screen or even on the 70-mm screen at the Cinerama on Sunset and Vine, something so colossal that it wouldn't even fit into the twentieth century itself. I wanted the Truth. For even then, I realized that chaos must be faced and the Truth must be told. And I knew that this would necessitate a very long journey—all the way from the Same to the Other, from a place called the Profane to a space called the Sacred.

1

Meeting Cartouche

The three-decked steamship had been following the contour of the palm-lined Indian coastline since sunrise, weaving its way through flotillas of fishing boats and other small ships until it reached Bombay. The voyage from Karachi was the final leg of a six-month overland journey that had taken me from Amsterdam to what would become my new home.

A deck-class ticket bought you a place on the ship but not a seat, berth, or cabin. You were on your own when it came to claiming a piece of the deck, usually the size of your straw mat or blanket. The two upper decks soon became a multicolored sea of bedding and people. When I first came aboard, Sigi, a young German, led me to a remote corner of the deck, where I could smell incense and there was a casbah partitioned with pastel silks into passageways and small camps. This, apparently, was the foreigners' quarter.

We were pilgrims, refugees, children of the revolution! We came from North America, South America, Asia, the Middle East, and every country in Europe. We had encountered one another at every stop along the way—Istanbul, Ankara, Konya, Tabriz, Tehran, Mashad, Herat, Kandahar, Kabul, Peshawar, Karachi—individuals, groups, and clans, all making the great pilgrimage. Where to? We were on our way home, moving toward the Light, or so we believed.

"Watch out for thieves," my new friend warned, as we put down our mats at the edge of the little colony. "It's usually the French. One of us must guard our belongings at all times."

"Pardon," said an orange-robed European with flowing black locks, accompanied by several young women. He resembled one of the three musketeers, except for his pointed Aladdin slippers. "You are going to *Inde-ia* for the *fairst* time?" he asked, introducing himself as Cartouche. "May we join you?"

"What kinda name . . ." I started.

"Egyptian," he said, "from my father's side. My mother is French."

He instructed the Pakistani coolie where to put each bag in what appeared to be flawless Urdu, argued over the price, said something that made the man laugh, and then paid him.

"We wanted to share this journey with spiritual people," Cartouche said, as he explained why they had moved from the Italian section of the deck. Cartouche and the girls spread their bedding next to mine. "You and I must have met before," he said, "perhaps in a previous life?"

A man dressed in a green Afghan robe came over to harangue Cartouche in Italian and was the recipient of a long burst in the same tongue. Cartouche's scowl turned to a smile as he remarked, "I told him to fuck off in his own language, if he wanted to remain attached to the material world!"

Sigi was suspicious. "Why did the Italians force you to move?"

"They are Greens," replied Cartouche, "You know, Muslims, and they thought it inappropriate for a Hindu holy man to camp beside them. They are making a pilgrimage to the holy places of their Sufi saints before heading down to Goa."

"I'm going straight to Goa," said Sigi. "A night in Bombay at the Carlton, and the morning boat to paradise." He said that he had some kind of a problem in Germany, and didn't plan to return there for many years. Everyone seemed to be headed to Goa.

"This is actually what he wants." Cartouche's eyes flashed as he pulled a drawstring bag out of another drawstring bag out of a shoulder bag. With great reverence he removed a small statue of the god Shiva, wrapped in red silk. "Swat Valley, maybe one thousand years old," he explained. "He wanted to pay me shit! And he's not even a Hindu!"

"I'm going to find me a nice shack on the beach," said the German, carefully placing his valuables under a makeshift pillow.

"Me, I want to find the ice palace of the Mother of the World, where the gods and goddesses hang out," crooned one of Cartouche's young women from under her veil. She was high on something.

"And you, my friend," Cartouche turned to me with his infectious smile, "Where will you go?"

I thought for a moment, like a child about to enter an amusement park, before blurting out, "I'm not sure, maybe Goa, but I'm looking for something . . . I'm not sure what yet, but it's something that we've lost in the West. Yeh, I guess I'm also going to India to have my mind blown!"

"Not enough action in your, uh, San Franseesko? That's why you have come?" he asked with raised eyebrows.

"Well, actually, I think I've sort of been pulled here." I grinned.

"That's the case with all of us," he said. Cartouche had very old eyes in contrast to his youthful face and body. He looked about twenty-two years old, a few years older than me, but had the demeanor and maturity of a man at least a generation older.

I had dropped out of high school. I had questions they wouldn't or couldn't answer. I had other ideas, perhaps immature and incomplete, but compelling. I had lost my faith in them, but not lost faith. I thought of Eric Hofstadter's *Manifest Destiny* as a pack of lies. I wanted to go join up with the American Indians. But they were all dead.

"Where are you from?" I asked him.

"From Paris," he said.

"You were there in May, the one before last, for the Revolution?" I asked him.

"*Non,* I was in India at the Kumbh Mela, the largest spiritual gathering in the world, with my guru. The real revolution is to transform yourself, not society. If you can succeed, then society will follow. The world is fucked up, corrupted by capitalist elites, but we cannot hope to win any war on the material plane. Finding the Truth is the only way."

For many young people, the lines that existed between politics, spirituality, and lifestyle were faint, if they existed at all. We were wildly idealistic and naive. I told Cartouche that I wanted to find a treasure in India that would somehow make the world a better place.

"A better place?" Cartouche asked. "For whom? Is it Heaven that you wish to bring to Earth, or is it Earth you'd like to raise to Heaven? If it is the former, you are following a long line of failures. Ask Karl Marx. And my friends who made the Revolution of '68, one day they will rule France, but nothing will be any different."

Cartouche had crossed the line and made it to the other side. He was confident and authoritative. He seemed to know India well, so I asked him if he could give me a list of places to visit.

"A waste of time," he replied. "You'll find all the right places. That's how India works."

"And what's with this 'ice palace'?" I asked, feeling a bit stupid. "Come on, is it a real place?"

"Sure it is," he said, "but you can't go there. Foreigners aren't allowed. It's in the Himalayas, within what they call the inner circle, too close to China. I guess they're afraid of spies."

"Have you been there?" I asked.

"*Non,* but I tried. The police caught me and sent me back down the mountain. My guru had told me that if I would meet him there, he would give me a magic potion that would let me live forever."

The small group that had been listening to our conversation dwindled until Cartouche and I were alone watching the moon sail across the sky. He enchanted me with more stories about his experiences in India. For as long as I could remember, I had been fascinated by what, in those days, we called the *occult.* I wanted to meet real shamans and wizards. I believed they existed, but I needed proof. I wanted to find ancient manuscripts containing secret knowledge, mantras, and spells. But that was all surface stuff. I desperately needed some answers. There were the basic questions concerning the meaning of life, death, after death, and Truth, and there were other less formulated questions that had arisen after I had taken mind-altering substances. In America I had been unable to find a Don Juan to guide me, but my omnivorous reading of the Upanishads, Vedanta, and books on Theosophy led me to believe that I could indeed find these answers in India.

"Don't waste your time going to Goa, hanging out with hippies. In India there are real masters that can teach the Path and help us understand who we are. The first thing you have to know before you begin your search is that there *is* no search, you are already *there* at that place where you hope to arrive, but it takes time to discover that. So, with that in mind, go and search," he said.

"But, where should I start?" I asked.

"Hey, enlightenment is not subject to the illusions of time and space. The possibility of transforming consciousness lies only in the here and now, but I'll give you some addresses," he replied.

He drew the Sanskrit character *Om* at the top of one of the pages in my notebook, explaining that this symbol would ensure the success of my quest. Then he wrote the names of a few temples and holy places and those of some of the big gurus. He explained which temples were dedicated to the Mother Goddess, which to Shiva, and which to the blue god Krishna. He rambled on about the claims and the feats of various teachers, including Satya Sai Baba, who could remember his past lives and materialize objects out of thin air, and then gave me the names and addresses of some sadhus, characterizing each as he wrote.

The last name was of a sadhu in Rajasthan. "Hari Puri Baba is a bit more modern. He speaks English, which my baba doesn't. I studied with my guru the traditional way, in Hindi and Sanskrit. Still, they say Hari Puri Baba is a *gyani,* a Knower. They say he knows how to read the world," Cartouche laughed. "Perhaps you would prefer to follow the Path in your mother tongue. Ah, if only the whole world spoke English, no?" He could be very sarcastic.

It was difficult for Cartouche to mask his contempt of Anglo-American culture. He was a spiritual Che Guevara, more so than I understood at the time. He made it clear that I would have to go native if I wanted to experience the real thing. He suggested that I buy a copy of *The Universal Hindi Teacher* as soon as I landed.

2

I Dream India into Existence

Clutching my diary and passport and with the rest of my worldly possessions slung over my shoulder in a small embroidered bag from Turkey, I walked down the gangplank into a new world whose sheer scale astounded me. I had never seen so many people in one place. There were colors I had never dreamed of and all around me new smells, new sounds, and seething activity. I stood there with my mouth open, trying to take it all in. I wanted to dive headfirst into the swirling colors.

Instead, I pushed my way through the unyielding crowd of white-capped men in white shirts and pajamas and women in saris of every color and design clinging to their sisters or the hands of children without pants. When I emerged from the long lines of immigration and customs to the street, I was surrounded by hustlers offering me "cycle rickshaw," "cheap hotel," "taxi," "change money," "hashish," "palm-reading," "best tailor," "cheap tickets," "opium den," and "he can grant your any wish." I examined the card the owner of the last voice had handed me. On it was a picture of a scruffy-looking man with a short white beard and white gown. "Baba," he said, before he was swept away.

"Baba," I repeated to myself. I liked the sound of it. It had a bounce, a primitive rhythm. Even though I didn't understand exactly what it meant, its onomatopoeic quality rang out to me. It was like "papa," but gentler. It seemed intimate yet possessed authority. I knew of Meher Baba, whose enigmatic smile was captioned "Don't worry, be happy." I had seen the bearded Mustan Baba on posters in the Haight Ashbury in the sixties, and read about the ageless Baba Ji in Paramahansa Yogananda's *Autobiography of a Yogi*. The card that had been thrust into my hand seemed both a talisman and a signpost.

I changed my last twenty dollars into rupees and, to conserve my meager resources, I hitchhiked, traveled ticketless on trains (and sometimes got thrown off), and walked. I slept in temples, ashrams, on the ground in railroad stations, and ate whatever I was offered. I visited holy places, cities, mountains, jungles, and famous landmarks. But it was the common people everywhere that touched me—their openness, their hospitality, their curiosity, their generosity. I began to fall in love with the land and its inhabitants.

I experienced the euphoria of total freedom, a sense of unlimited possibilities. On any given day I imagined myself to be a gypsy, an Arabian knight, a maharaja. I quickly discarded my sturdy shoes for pointed slippers, my pants for striped pajamas, and my shirts for knee-length kurtas. I tied my long blond hair into a topknot. As I worked through my fantasies, I exchanged my slippers for sandals, and eventually opted for bare feet. Pajamas gave way to *lungis*, sarongs, and as I wandered further south, into the heat, I abandoned my kurtas and went bare-chested, a light turban protecting my head from the sun.

I dreamed India into existence. Not that it was my personal private dream, but a believable movie reasonably constructed from the group psyche. It was comforting this dream, cushioned, as it were, with familiarity. It tamed the wild profusion of things, using the sights, sounds, and faces of India as its raw material. Everything might appear different from my ordinary world back home, but I knew that this was the way it was supposed to be. It was a good dream, it made me feel happy.

I recognized India immediately, like meeting a blood relative for the first time, because I carried with me, deep inside, images corresponding to what I saw on the outside. Later I realized that these images resembled Orientalist paintings of nineteenth-century Europe. I saw that same domed dwelling as the artist Delamain. I learned to label it a *dargah,* the tomb of a Sufi saint. I searched the back streets of the Muslim Quarter looking for Deutsch's water seller, knowing full well I would never drink that water. Guaranteed dysentery. But I *would* enter into his doorways.

I dreamed the Orient, fueled on these images and others that filtered their way down a hundred years into my thoughts. By their circuitous expansion into popular culture, into literature and film, I was informed, prepared. I was ready for the sensuality, promise, terror, spirituality, delight, and intense energy that I had been promised. Thoughts appeared in my head that led me to compare and contrast normal with abnormal, the Same with the Other, and to assign categories to my experience of India: what it was supposed to be.

But I was unable to understand then that there was another India right under my feet and before my eyes, an India that was different from my dream. I did not grasp that my idea of India told me more about my own culture, and how it imagined another culture than it did about this extraordinary land itself.

India gradually began to reveal itself as sacred geography. Mountains were no longer masses of inert granite observing the laws man assigns to nature but living beings—gods and sages. Rivers became goddesses. I started to recognize everywhere the signs of these great beings, the spectacular signatures of nature. How else would we know where the great powers of the universe reside, how else would we know the meeting of worlds, if these places were not clearly marked? This topography is known throughout India in a voluminous mythological narrative, often conflicting, and confusing to me, but as such, the very source of mystery and wonder. I discovered that there were those who read the face of this Extraordinary World with its flags, characters, ciphers, and obscure words the way we read a book.

When I started out, I had no guidebook or map and knew nothing of the lay of the land. The diary that I had kept since Amsterdam quickly filled up with names, places, and accounts of what I saw and heard. Wherever I went, I would learn of three or four more places to check out. I slept with it under my head and each night I looked through my notes for someone or some place that might be *it*. It? *The* place, *the* person, the key that would unlock the hidden language. The information Cartouche had given me formed a general outline. I traveled south, all the way to what was then called Trivandrum but is now Tiruvanathapuram, then slowly headed north again toward the Himalayas.

I would set off to visit temples and holy men at a moment's notice on the basis of a hot tip. I went to Puttaparti to see Satya Sai Baba, Ganeshpuri to see Baba Muktananda, Rishikesh to see Tatwala Baba, Varanasi to see Neelakanth Tata Ji, and Ananda Mayi Ma, as well as other luminaries on the way. They were all very impressive, especially Ananda Mayi Ma, a true living goddess. They all spoke of knowing oneself and the Truth, and there was something so familiar about their words that came to me in translation, something that resonated with what I already knew. At each stop I would ask myself whether I should become a disciple, but I always moved on within the day. I collected blessings but despite the authenticity and stature of these teachers, none of them blew me away, and that was what I was seeking. Besides, I always felt like an outsider in their ashrams.

I told myself that the small inconsistencies and irritations that might manifest were masala, or spice. India was supposed to be dirty, of course there were beggars, and hustling was just a way of life. These things didn't interfere with the dream but enhanced it. Potential allies would approach me from the street, from ashrams. They knew I was dreaming, and they were patronizing. Anything you want, they would say. Just pay the price of admission—and my 10 percent. Just a couple of bucks.

I felt the power, the eye of holy men fell on me when I passed them at temples, on the road, and at bus terminals, and I felt it pulling me, as if reclaiming a missing child. Their hair matted, beards down to their waists, they would call me over, offer me tea, and, more often than not, a smoke. Sometimes marijuana, which they called *ganja,* or hashish, which they called *charas,* but always mixed with the tobacco of a cigarette, and smoked in a *chillam,* a cylindrical clay pipe which widens at the top.

I learned to call these ascetics *sadhus* and *sannyasis.* Swathed in ochre cloth as a flag of their renunciation, they looked like the deities I saw in temples. People touched their feet and offered them sweets, flowers, and money. Yet I also sensed that they were marginal characters, proud of their distance from society, dropouts like me. They seemed to operate under a different set of rules. I sensed a kinship with them: The rules I had grown up with had lost their meaning, and my own goals varied from those of my society.

The fact that they had some special knowledge brought out a hip arrogance in these sadhus. Their eyes twinkled, and I found their electricity magnetic. But there was a huge difference between us: They seemed to Know, and I didn't. They all shared some secret, and I wanted to know whatever it was they knew. I wanted in, but I didn't even have the categories in which to put these people who were more storybook than real.

I learned that these sadhus and sannyasis lived in temples, caves, thatched huts, and in monastery-like retreats called ashrams. Sometimes they spent their lives wandering the jungles and mountains. They also practiced various spiritual techniques and disciplines called *sadhana* (hence sadhu) or Yoga. A sadhu who formalized his renunciation through a fabulous yet terrifying initiation ritual was called a *sannyasi,* or "he who has given up everything."

The sadhus that I met all over India emulated and worshipped Shiva, the great ascetic god of the Hindus. I began to notice this god everywhere. In pictures, posters, and statues, Shiva is usually depicted as a long-haired, three-eyed, effeminate-looking man, ash-white in color, sitting in deep meditation on a tiger skin, two eyes rolled upward and the third one closed. He wears a cobra around his neck and the five-day-old crescent moon in his hair from which a torrent of water (the Ganges or Ganga) springs forth. In his hand he holds a trident, with a two-headed drum dangling from its spikes. The great bull, Nandi, waits on him and serves as his divine vehicle. This naked ascetic, the great god Shiva, roams the three worlds (Heaven, Earth, and Hell) in ecstatic bliss. He is the first baba.

Because his meditative state of pure consciousness is considered to be the very foundation of the universe, the prerequisite for creation, Shiva is worshipped as a phallus. In his temples, this phallus, called a *Shiva linga,* usually takes the form of a large, naturally polished, egg-shaped stone, preferably coming from the Narmada River that flows east to west through central India.

I became enchanted listening to stories of gods, yogis, shamans, and other sometimes-bizarre sages. I heard of sadhus performing great austerities, acquiring superhuman powers, called *siddhis,* attaining great wisdom and the highest levels of consciousness. Every devotee had stories of superhuman feats that his guru had accomplished. There was Shri Shri Shri Sivabalayogi, who had remained in perfect yogic absorption for twenty or thirty years, not eating or speaking, and barely breathing. He appeared in public once a year, during the rites of Shiva, when the doors of the temple in which he sat were pulled open. There was Baba Ji, about whom Yogananda wrote. He was hundreds of years old, could appear at several places at the same time, and transport himself in a flash anywhere he wanted to go. There were those who could fly, travel to other dimensions, sit naked all winter on a glacier, enter the bodies of others, heal the sick, and raise the dead. There were those who knew the Truth. I wanted to meet these extraordinary men and women, and to understand and experience just what the human possibilities in this Extraordinary World were.

I wanted to know my own possibilities, who I was, and where I belonged. I had to find someone who knew, and who could and would tell me. I was desperate to know how I fit into the cosmic scheme of things. I was determined to find my very own Dharma, my correct path, as I continued to wander through India, looking for clues and ready for anything.

However, I had a language problem. Yes, English is a major language in India. It is spoken everywhere and is the mother language of many Indians. One can easily get by in English anywhere in the Indian subcontinent, except with sadhus. Of course, one can communicate, English or no English, as one can all over the world with aware or awakened people. But in an Extraordinary World, where metaphor may drive reality, when esoteric instruction is as precise as a computer program, comprehension and articulation in the sage's own language is highly desirable. Among the traditional sadhus, yogis, and shamans I met, none spoke English. This was not surprising, but I found it extremely frustrating. I had started to learn Hindi but feared that it would take years before I could have a real conversation with or take instruction from one of these adepts.

My first three months in India went by very quickly. As my visa was about to expire, I decided to go to Delhi where I would either find a way to extend it or travel to Nepal and obtain a new one there. I met a young sadhu while waiting for the train in Nasik, north of Bombay. We struck up a quick friendship and managed to communicate despite the fact that neither of us had command of the other's language. What we did have in common was our long hair.

Thumping himself on the chest, and shaking the dreadlocks that hung halfway down his back, he called himself a Naga Baba, a yogi. *Naga* means "naked," and indeed many Naga Babas have abandoned all clothing, but to these yogis, their initiation into nakedness meant that they had given up everything of the Ordinary World, including its social behavior, rules, rituals, and books. I saw them as the Hell's Angels of babas.

The young baba, who wore only an ochre cloth around his waist, couldn't have even been my age, which was nineteen at the time, as he was failing miserably in his attempt to grow a mustache out of peach fuzz. He was going to see his guru in Ujjain, one of the most ancient and sacred cities in India. "I am nothing," he said, "but my guru is everything." So I decided to postpone my Delhi trip and accompany him instead. How could I pass up this opportunity?

When we arrived, the young baba took me to the simple Shiva temple where he lived with his guru and several other sadhus. A great tree spread out over much of the courtyard protecting it from the scorching rays of the sun. His brash behavior melted away in front of his guru, and he became the boy that he was and went right to work. I was enjoying the company of his guru, an old laughing

Buddha of a man, but the young baba, after touching his master's feet, and offering a small box of sweets with a coin on top, quickly departed to the kitchen area to prepare vegetables.

"Here? There? Where you will go?" the old baba asked me in his broken English. He waved his hand in a circle. I knew what he meant. I was running around like a chicken without a head. If I hadn't wanted "in" as much as I did, I might not have felt so outside and could have enjoyed the exotic locale as a spiritual tourist. I felt a subtle shift in my perception. There were doorways, passageways, in my dream of India, whose entrances had proved inaccessible. Could I dream my way through the labyrinth? Perhaps. But I sensed I needed some additional tools. *It requires a leap,* I thought.

After sunset, evening worship began. Two babas, standing in the temple, banged brass plates with wooden mallets, alternating two beats each, a tempo that started to sound like the rhythm of time. The old baba looked at his watch, he shook it a few times, and looked at it again, then he put it to his ear. Obviously it wasn't working.

Helped by two of the younger babas, the old one got on his feet and led us over to the temple. We walked up a couple of steps through medieval archways into the *mandapa,* or meeting hall, where already half-dozen babas had gathered and were ringing the heavy gunmetal bells hanging down from the ceiling on long chains in front of the holy of holies, the inner temple housing the Shiva linga. The smoke from the incense and wood resins created a haze in the hall. I strained to see the priest pouring water on the Shiva linga and then decorating it with flowers. The crowd swelled, another dozen enthusiastic babas had arrived. The baba-priest now waved a brass butter lamp, five wicks and five flames, in circles in front of the linga, while a couple of drummers whacked their *dholak* drums.

I stood on tiptoe behind the frenzied worshippers so that I could watch the priest, his head swaying to the hypnotic beat, offering Fire to the god Shiva. I tried to get closer, but everyone had the same idea; the crowd surged. The pulsating sounds were overpowering, pulling me like an ocean riptide, filling my veins with liquid rhythm. I began to lose control and tried to resist.

Then I caught myself. What was I doing? Why fight it? Let go! My eyes closed for a moment, and my body starting swaying to the percussion—brass plates banged, bells jangled, and drums cracked. I felt myself dancing. I opened my eyes to see the crowd give way before me. I moved slowly forward, rising up from the temple floor with every step, a few inches at first, and then I was dancing on air. Soon I began to float, supine, four or five feet above the ground. I was able to put my head just inside the holy of holies, which had a low arch, and saw five little fire deities, little Agnis, dancing in front of Shiva in the form of a large egg of naturally polished black stone. The wet black stone radiated heat that made me sweat, and it made a sound like *Om* that hummed louder and louder until it consumed all the other sounds. Maybe it *was* the Mother of all Sounds.

Everything was suddenly very quiet, and I became aware that there was nothing holding me up. At the same time I realized that I was no longer attached to my body, and I fell to the ground with a great crash.

Hara Hara Mahadev!

They were shouting,

Hara Hara Mahadev!

When I was able to focus again, I saw the heavy round jowls of the old baba who was cradling me. Ten faces looked down at me with concern.

Hara Hara Mahadev!

They kept shouting as the old baba made me sniff some more camphor. I tried getting up but was too weak to move.

"What happened?" I asked.

"Shiva like you," smiled the old man.

When I finally gathered my wits about me, it seemed likely that I had passed out just where I had been standing. It had all become too much for me—the noise, the excitement, and my exhaustion from traveling. But, I *had* left my body and entered into another state of consciousness.

The next morning I felt so foolish about what I had done the night before that I wanted to leave immediately for Delhi. I bathed from a bucket next to the hand pump, and sat with the old baba for a few minutes. We had tea, and when I got up to leave, he took me by surprise by giving me a strange gift. He placed a railroad ticket from Ujjain to Jaipur in my hand.

The young baba, with whom I had arrived, shouldered my small bag and walked me to the station. Waiting for the train, I pulled out my diary, and wrote down his address and learned his name for the first time. I also paged back to Cartouche's notes from the ship, which seemed a lifetime ago. Cartouche had said that Hari Puri Baba lived in an ashram in the state of Rajasthan, near Jaipur. It was time to meet him.

3

Hari Puri Baba

My dream of India fully matured in Rajasthan, the land of kings. Leaving the pink city of Jaipur, the bus entered the scrub desert heading north on the Bikaner Road, negotiating right-of-way with camel caravans, camel carts, and the odd camel napping in the middle of the highway. I held on tightly to the rusted railing of the seat in front of me as we bounced and jerked our way toward Chaumun. The dreamscape of this land appearing through the dusty haze conjured up Arabian Nights or Lawrence of Arabia. The Arravali Hills rose up on both sides of the road, and I could see ancient red stone forts, mostly in ruins, lining the ridges, once powerful military outposts, now monuments to the noble race of Rajput warriors. *I've finally arrived,* I thought.

Cartouche had given me accurate directions. When I reached Chaumun, I took an even older and more broken-down bus to Samod, which was clearly the end of the line. High above the village, scattered along the base of the rocky hillside, was the grand palace of the Rawal of Samod, built on three levels and surrounded by a red stone wall. I was now beyond passable roads, electricity, and telephones, and walked on a footpath through a medieval India of crumbling ruins, mud villages, straw-roofed huts, small stone temples, and rock outcrops.

In Rajasthan, color and combinations of colors tease the senses and reach higher levels of esthetics than anywhere else in India. The simple village women, weighed down with silver jewelry and thick silver ankle bracelets, wore brilliant oranges, electric blues, blushing pinks, robust reds, and vibrant rice-paddy greens. The men's oversized tie-dyed or red-maroon-magenta polka-dot turbans shielded their faces, which were dry and cracked like the earth from the powerful desert sun. Their brightly painted earthen houses and piles of drying ox-blood red chile peppers stood out in contrast to the barren burnt land.

The footpath to the village of Amloda was packed with festive villagers all walking in the same direction. Must be some action somewhere ahead, I thought: a festival or a cricket match. I passed *chhatris,* cenotaphs, domed umbrellas supported by stone pillars, built to commemorate great warriors as well as their dutiful wives who sacrificed themselves on their husbands' funeral pyres. The crowd thickened as I reached Amloda.

A wedding band, in their Salvation Army–like rag-tag uniforms, shuffled along the small main square playing their bubble-gum marching music with trumpets, trombones, clarinets, and a snare drum—a Western institution gone native. I asked where I could find Hari Puri Baba and was told that he was in the field to the west, where a large crowd had gathered.

I meandered through the music, dance, puppetry, and magic, asking from time to time for Hari Puri Baba. I got vague answers, heads jerking left or right indicating "somewhere over there." Did anyone really know? Eventually I was directed to the sacrificial area surrounding the sacred fire, where twelve Brahmin priests were performing *havan,* fire sacrifice. Smoke billowed out from the raised enclosure with a large sloping bamboo and thatched roof. One of the *pandit*-priests beamed at me. Later I learned that this was Pandit Shesh Narayan, maker of babas.

A number of villagers touched my feet, smiled, and looked at me with reverence as I stood there watching the oblations of ghee, sesame seeds, dried coconut, fragrant resinous wood, sticks, and twigs, go into the fire. The harmonious chanting of Vedic mantras gave me a sense of well-being. A couple of Brahmins placed garlands of marigolds around my neck. How welcoming and hospitable these people are, I thought. Pandit Shesh Narayan greeted me and invited me to sit at the sacrifice. I thanked him, but told him I was looking for Hari Puri Baba. He pointed halfway up the hill on the other side of the village. "Guru Ji," he said, "there."

I looked up at the hill and was shocked by what I saw. How can I describe it without risking that you will think me perverted? But I do feel obligated to tell you, for what I saw was so vivid, that, despite rubbing my eyes twice, and cleaning my glasses, it remains in my mind's eye to this day. From the bare rocky hill emerged the open thighs of a giant woman, her pubic hair the only greenery on the mountain. I tried unsuccessfully to banish the thought that arose in my mind: I have come to meet a celibate hermit who lives in the private parts of a great rock woman.

I climbed the hill on a path of large stones, and as I got closer, I saw that the lady's pubic hair was mango trees. When I arrived at the threshold, an oasis appeared before me: it was a "meeting of worlds." The gateway was made from bamboo decorated with sugar-cane stalks, fruit-laden branches hewn from a banana tree, green coconuts, marigolds, sparkly colored foils, and fire-engine red cloth. I watched two turbaned villagers march through it. As I entered I saluted the emaciated sadhu who sat there on an old blanket.

"Hey you!"

My further progress was obstructed by the baba puffing on a clay chillam. He wore only a *lingoti*, a loincloth. "Hey!!" he shouted again, barring the entrance. I explained to him as best I could that I wanted to see Swami Hari Puri Baba; I was in the right place, wasn't I? "Who?" he asked, as he held a matchbox between his toes, struck a match, and fired up his chillam, blowing the smoke through his nostrils. I repeated Hari Puri Baba's name a couple of times until he acknowledged that I was indeed in the right place. The interrogation then took the form of sign language. My Hindi was still weak, and the baba had no teeth. I told him I had come from America, and putting my hands together, and bowing my head, I told him I wanted to pay my respects to Hari Puri Baba. "*Thik hai!* good," he said, but before I could enter, he again put his hand up. "Ticket?" he demanded. "Ticket?" I asked. You've got to be kidding. "Ha . . . ticket!" he demanded again, putting out his hand. "Oh!" I understood. Reaching into my bag, I dropped a small ball of hashish into his hand. "Go!" he said.

From a distance, I saw the ochre-clad baba sitting erect, even proud, atop a large wooden platform, a *takht,* about the size of a raised queen-size bed facing sideways. He was waving his hands, crafting something out of the air, as he addressed some naked sadhus covered in ashes that made them look like ghosts. Their hair was matted in long dreadlocks, *jatas,* untamed and unruly like the vines of the banyan tree. Hari Puri Baba himself was well groomed, his thinning black hair tied neatly in a knot on the back of his head, his sparse beard tied beneath his chin. His long mustache spread wide across his face in a smile, and three horizontal lines of mustard-colored sandalwood paste dotted with a pair of red *bindu*s marked his long forehead. A sign of wisdom, I thought.

Hari Puri Baba sat like a general on his tiger skin, his fragile body appearing much larger than it actually was. He shared his throne with a much larger sadhu, whom I learned later was Amar Puri Baba. He was equally well groomed but made himself smaller out of love for his *guru bhai,* his spiritual brother. As different as two men were in looks and temperament, they could have been twins. Raising both hands, Hari Puri Baba silenced his rowdy troops as I approached. Six ghost faces turned toward me and six jaws dropped. Had they never seen a foreigner before? They looked me up and down, as did Hari Puri Baba. Amar Puri Baba squinted. He was suspicious. Hari Puri Baba leaned forward and fingered one of the tiger claws.

"Baba Ji, are you Swami Hhharrr . . ." I started to ask him with sixteen eyes fixed on my every movement.

"Of course I am," he interrupted me in perfect English, "You came here to see me, no? So? So what you want?"

I knew what I wanted, but the question caused my mind to go blank. There was a murmur and a clatter among the assembled ghosts. A fat one growled at me. Another rose, put his ashen face next to mine, and repeatedly raised his eyebrows, trying to get a response. I couldn't help but notice that he had a silver ring on his penis. Amar Puri Baba frowned. "You don't speak Hindi?" Hari Puri Baba asked.

"I came for your *darshan,*" I said, my voice shaking and my face burning. He stared down at me and pulled the black hairs on his chin. Something was happening here that I hadn't experienced before. I felt as though I was on stage and paranoid about forgetting my lines or called upon in the classroom when I hadn't done my homework. These men seemed like a jury, closely examining everything I said or did. Only moments ago, Hari Puri Baba had been just a name among many in my notebook. Suddenly, a face, a body, a voice, but most of all a particular presence claimed that name.

I touched his feet, as I was now accustomed to do when meeting holy men, but this time a heavy weight pushed my head down, and then someone's forehead touched his toes. It was my forehead, because I felt a pat, a caress, on the back of my head. I didn't look up but moved back slowly. The holy ghosts shook their heads, "no," which in India means "yes."

Ah, the other baba, the frowning one, yes, him, too. I touched Amar Puri Baba's right foot. Hari Puri Baba invited me to sit on his right, sackcloth appeared on the ground under me, and I took my seat. One by one, each baba put his head to Hari Puri Baba's foot and held it in both hands, and then each slipped a banknote, I think a ten-rupee bill, and a rupee coin under his thigh. Hari Puri Baba noticed my curiosity. "It's just a little bet I had with the *bhuts,* the ghosts. I won," he said.

"And why have you come so far to meet an old madman like me?" he asked, "Or is it that you just came for the waters?" He laughed and pointed to the *kund,* the spring, enshrined with carved boulders probably placed there by giants. Five stone steps led down to the pool that bubbled up from deep inside the mountain. Stone icons of gods and goddesses faced the spring from ledges just above the surface of the sparkling waters. It must be the lost fountain of youth, I thought. "From her comes life," Hari Puri Baba said.

"Actually, Baba Ji, I've come to India to find a teacher," I said, suddenly aware that I was also being observed by a gang of skinny silver langur monkeys in the mango trees.

"What? A teacher? There are many kinds," he replied.

"I want to know my self," I said.

"Okay, that's easy," said Hari Puri Baba. "Sit with your back straight and breathe. Yes, breathe in and out. That's it. You didn't have to come all the way from England to learn that!" he laughed. They all laughed, not knowing why.

"America, Baba Ji," I corrected him.

"Oh, America, Germany, France, Malaya! What else do you want to know?" he asked.

I could say nothing.

"Good," Hari Puri Baba said, "then I want to welcome you to the sacred grove of the goddess Amloda!"

Although no one else present spoke English, they all leaned forward to listen when his barrage of questions began. The first question is always "Where are you coming from?" An ambiguous loaded question; so its very weight makes it the leading one. But this was just the beginning. He wanted to know everything about me. He studied me when I spoke. It surprised him that I was American. "I thought you would be English," he said. What did Hari Puri Baba mean by that? When did he think I would be English, I wondered. He thought it very strange that despite the fact I was American, my native language was English and not "American." He told me that he hadn't even considered the possibility of learning "American." Was I missing something?

Although I didn't have a clue as to what was going on in this strange place, my language was just too weak, I continued to notice oddities and seeming inconsistencies. Amidst the serving of chai, being garlanded again by two Brahmins, and the incessant banter, I kept hearing myself referred to by the word "rampuri." I didn't know what it meant. The mood became very jovial, and I only wished I could understand the jokes that Hari Puri Baba must have been telling to keep the crowd laughing.

I asked him about the occasion for the festival. He evidently translated my question for the others, which made them laugh again. He tilted his head on one side and asked, "What? You don't know? No one told you?"

Hari Puri Baba's cavernous dark eyes and nose ruled his face; his mouth was barely visible as his mustache covered most of what was left. "He had the face of a mongoose but the eyes of a fox," I heard Amar Puri Baba describe Guru Ji years later.

"Look about you! And look down there," he said, pointing to the large crowd. "You see sadhus, no? Look how many Brahmins have come. Many have come from as far away as Ujjain, and further. You see they make *yajna,* Vedic fire sacrifice. And see the public, Ram Puri Ji. See how many hundreds and hundreds of simple people are here. It is a great occasion!"

There were ochre banners and other flags of many colors. Everywhere I went, I had seen flowers, flower *malas,* flower petals, and sellers of flowers. There was fresh whitewash on the temple. Itinerant bards sang vernacular songs but could barely be heard through the din of the wedding band and the crackling PA system that screeched and whined devotional songs from Hindi films. Ever-present drums maintained a hypnotic rhythm, suggesting tribal roots. There were sellers of herbs, magic potions, and animal claws. High-ranking policemen wandered about, off duty, in starched uniforms; and Rajasthani turbans everywhere contributed to the rainbow sea.

"Come inside," said Hari Puri Baba, standing up. He led me to a room in the ashram and sat down on a wooden bed with a cotton mattress. He had me sit on the floor on an old burlap sack at his feet. One of the babas brought in a container of hot milk. Hari Puri Baba poured us each a cup. He pulled a gaily-decorated box off the shelf behind him, and put three rich sweetmeats on a plate for me.

"It's too much for me, Baba Ji," I said.

"Eat them all. You're much too skinny. I can see you haven't been eating well," he said frowning and showing a mother's concern. "Health is good? Happy, blissful? Good."

I searched him for signs. Was this wisdom? Was this enlightenment that I saw in Hari Puri Baba's eye? I wasn't sure. He sits with a very straight back, I thought, almost like a statue. His feet were calloused and cracked from many journeys. My eyes darted quickly around the room. The wall had an old rusty saber hanging on it, crooked. Why a sword? Maybe a symbol of knowledge?

"What's the sword for, Baba Ji?" I asked.

"Chopping off British heads!" he said on the beat, raising his hand and then slicing the air with cruel authority. "We are simple babas, but even simple babas can be dangerous," he said, twisting the end of his moustache, his eyes wide. "We don't play by the rules."

I thought I would be able to recognize a realized being. I thought I would have that sudden moment of recognition, as if from a past life or of a father one has never seen. I thought he might have a long white beard and hold a lotus flower in his hand.

"We could spend a lot of time getting to know each other and, in the process, we could test each other. I could test you to determine whether or not you might become a fruitful disciple, and you in your clumsy way could test me as a competent guru. I'm not interested in all that," he said.

Amar Puri Baba entered the room and sat on the bed next to Hari Puri Baba. He examined every inch of me and then fastened his stare on me like a cat, reacting to my every movement.

"You see," he continued, "I know how you got that bump on your head!" He laughed as I touched the slight ridge hidden by my hair. "I don't know you, but I know all about you," he said. "I read the world. It's all written in the signs and, for some reason, God has made me literate.

"You, of course, want to know if I can teach you the secrets of the soul, the *atma vidya,* you want to know if I can show you who you really are, no? That's why you came.

"Our tradition maintains the qualifications of a guru. The first is that since the guru has crossed over death and rebirth, he has the capacity to lead others along the same path. How do you know where I've been?

"In the case of the spiritual seeker who pursues knowledge of Brahman, which is the knowledge of the Self, a close personal association between the guru and disciple is established. The goal of such a relationship is transformation whereby the student, after his self-realization, becomes a guru himself.

"*Shastra* is the only source of the knowledge of the truths regarding what is beyond the senses. What do I mean by *Shastra*? You would probably translate it as scripture or text, but I'm talking about a different kind of text from what you are used to. It is not written; it's not a book. This is text that goes way off the page, way beyond its front and back covers. Yes, you can print the mantras and the other sounds. You can print some version of the story, but its authority and power lie in the empty spaces. On the paper these are the white spaces that haven't been touched by ink. The printing can be perceived from as many different perspectives as there are people and spirits and gods. The text is the tradition manifested through its knower."

One by one the babas crept into the room. They sat on the ground with no sacking underneath them after they had touched Hari Puri Baba's feet. "I did that to them," Hari Puri Baba said proudly. "I made them naked."

One of the babas tugged at my shoulder bag, trying to pry it away from me. When I turned around, a little irritated, Hari Puri Baba told the young man, whom he addressed as Kedar Puri, to behave himself.

"The knowledge that leads to liberation can be achieved through traditional authority, and that authority comes through a line of teachers. Traditional authority is the way of effectively passing down knowledge through time. There is no pursuit of wisdom independent of one's gurus. In this way, the path is the goal. In our tradition the guru is the patron of the disciple, willing to travel to any of the three worlds to save his rear end."

I began to see Hari Puri Baba as my highest aspiration. He was what I might become if I persisted on the Path of Heroes.

But, why couldn't I figure out everything by myself? Because the most advanced men and women of every generation try this with greater or lesser success, but Nature maintains codes and languages, to transmit information from generation to generation. A tradition is what enables one to follow the path, to search for identity and meaning, as part of a collective soul disqualifying time as a barrier. Without the benefit of a tradition, one must start from scratch and go through countless lifetimes of building a way of seeing and knowing. You still have to figure it all out yourself. You must find the path and walk on it. The guru can point the way, help you cross some thresholds, train you, punish you, rescue you, and ultimately give you blessings. You, however, must do the walking.

Just a minute. Am I in danger here? Is my soul being lured into realms of trial by this mercurial being, rational and irrational, protective yet dangerous, motherly and fatherly all at the same time?

"You really don't know the reason for today's festivities?" Hari Puri Baba asked. His voice became intoxicating. "This is your welcoming," he said flatly. A smile spread over his face. "This is all for you, celebrating your arrival here."

Even though not one of the sadhus understood English, they all seemed to agree. They kept nodding their heads from side to side. Was I being taken, as I had been several times in the bazaars? I started feeling dizzy and a bit nauseous, and it had nothing to do with the chillams that were going around.

"I have been waiting for you, I knew you would come today," he said. "Do you know what it means to be a disciple, a *chela*?" He didn't wait for my reply. "It means that you have a guide, a benefactor, a protector, one who will show you a path, and do everything in his power to see to it that you also cross to the other side, as he has, so that you may show the path to others and keep it from disappearing. Do you understand everything I am saying?"

I nodded.

"There is one more thing," he stated, his face darkening. "You must make a serious commitment. You must offer your life to the sacrifice of knowledge. You must leave the world of your birth, the material world, and enter the spiritual world of yogis and renunciates. You must leave all your baggage behind," he laughed.

"So you must make a formal request. Do you want me to make you my disciple?"

"Whoa, you've told me so much, Baba Ji. I'm just trying to understand it all. Let me think about it."

"No. It's now or never."

"Now," I said. I have always been able to make immediate decisions, even those that are important, like this one.

"Then, today, I will make you my chela, my disciple."

namah parvati pate
hara hara mahadev!

Hail to that Lord of the
Lady of the Mountain!
Hail to Shiva!

The naked babas acknowledged the words of Hari Puri Baba with praise to the great God Shiva.

Pandit Shesh Narayan, the Brahmin pandit who beamed at me from the havan, sat down behind me and gripped my shoulders as though I were a long-lost friend or family member. He was the pandit that performs the *Virja Havan,* the initiation ritual into *Sannyas* for every neophyte who enters the *Juna Akhara,* the Old

Order, and today he was presiding over the *Shiva-Shakti Yajna*.

I couldn't understand what the pandit was trying to tell me, not even the "rampuri, rampuri." I turned to Guru Ji who translated, "This most clever of men just said to you that you will be lucky to have me as your guru. Maybe you are very unlucky. Only God knows." He said nothing about the word, "rampuri."

Second thoughts arose. "I don't know if I'm ready for this," I protested. Why did it have to be now, at this moment? Perhaps I should really think about it for a few days, or maybe check out a few other gurus before I make any decision."

"You will never be ready for this," said Hari Puri Baba. "This is not something you or anyone else is ever ready for." He laughed, and I didn't know whether to take him seriously or not.

4

Becoming Rampuri

If I were a *rishi*-sage, a *suta*-bard, or some other ancient hearer or teller of tales, or even an overzealous devotee, I might say that when Hari Puri Baba was born, the gods and the goddesses rained fragrant flowers from heaven, cows tripled their flow of milk for a month, and for once, there was peace on Earth. But, no, I won't say that. I will give you only the facts. I will tell you that he was a far from ordinary child. He came from a Brahmin family, the royal astrologers to the kings of Mandi, in what is now Himachal Pradesh. An old traditional family, it passed the treasure trove of the knowledge of past and future as well as the timing and suitability of important events from father to son from at least the time of the Rishi Bhrigu, millennia ago. Kings from the four directions, yogis, scholars, and even great astrologers would come for consultation for the predictions and advice were infallible.

Hari Puri Baba's mother fainted when informed by her husband that their firstborn son would become a great sannyasi. Anything but that. She knew her husband had the power to counteract certain influences that could be interpreted from the heavens, and begged him to do something. Not that Hari Puri Baba's father wanted his son to become a sadhu, but he knew a baba when he saw one.

On the day of a lunar eclipse, when the world hides in fear inside their homes, Sandhya Puri Baba, the great and famous Siddha, a wizard who had accomplished superhuman yogic powers, came for consultation with Hari Puri Baba's father. On that day ten-year-old Hari Puri Baba's world changed. Enchanted by the baba, and always hardheaded, the boy decided to follow Sandhya Puri Baba. He didn't want to become an astrologer, telling other people what to do. He wanted to be free as the wind, wandering here and there, learning and practicing siddhis like Sandhya Puri Maharaj. His mother's tears couldn't stop him (his mother did, however, give him both permission and blessings to leave), and his father, impressed by Sandhya Puri Baba, reasoned that if his son were to be a sadhu, then at least he would be the disciple of a great saint.

Even by the time he left home, however, he had already achieved mastery over several intellectual/spiritual traditions in Sanskrit (including astrology), and was considered somewhat of a prodigy in language and mantra.

As a disciple, he trained under Sandhya Puri, wandering barefoot "hither and thither," as he would later say, throughout the Himalayas, in Kashmir, Punjab, Nepal, Yarkhand, Tibet, and other parts of what is now China. Sandhya Puri would take him for darshan, the auspicious seeing and meeting of other siddhas who lived and practiced austerities in high Himalayan caves. He would leave his young disciple there for a year at a time to perform *seva*, auspicious service, to the great ones.

This is the *guru shishya parampara*, the path of discipleship: Perform service to the guru, please him, and if you are lucky, then perhaps he will give you his blessing, an *ashirvad*. Let the ashirvad grow, and over decades a transmission takes place in which the disciple absorbs the Tradition as well as the personality of the guru. Please him a lot, and you may compel him to do your bidding, as humans have compelled gods, by pleasing them a lot, since story took birth.

Over the years, Hari Puri Baba obtained a number of siddhis. I knew him for only a short time and cannot vouch for whatever powers he might (or might not) have had, but I can attest to his great knowledge of language. Sanskrit and Indian languages, even Tamil, Telegu, and Maliyalam are one thing. His sophisticated "foreign-returned" sounding English is not rare in a country like India. The European languages—French, Italian, and Spanish—raised my eyebrows a little, even more when I heard him speak German, which he had picked up in less than a day. But when I saw him in conversation with crows, my order of things became disorderly. He spoke *Ka Bhasha* (crow language), the language of birds.

Until recently I never met another Naga Sannyasi of Juna Akhara, the Old Order, who spoke any English. It was a boon for me that my sharp transition into Hindi would be cushioned by the fact that my guru spoke my mother tongue.

In 1959, Hari Puri Baba visited the Bhrigu Shastri, a great astrologer, in Hosharpur, Punjab, who possessed the *Bhrigu Shastra,* a text composed thousands of years ago by the Rishi Bhrigu, his ancestor. The Bhrigu Shastri also has a highly guarded section of that ancient text, which contains horoscopes for those who would approach his lineage for thousands of years to come. He is able to find the horoscope for anyone who approaches him. He simply notes down the precise moment the client crosses the threshold of his simple house, makes a few calculations, and then starts poring through his palm leaf manuscripts, looking for that particular individual in his nonlinear chronology of horoscopes. Hari Puri Baba stayed with the Shastri for several weeks while they went through Baba Ji's life, as well as his past lives.

Baba Ji learned that he would have only three disciples. One would perish in a fire, one would lose his powers and eventually be murdered, and the third would be a foreigner. I asked Hari Puri Baba Ji several times what would happen to the foreigner, but he never told me. All he would say was that he knew the exact moment I would cross the threshold of his ashram at Amloda Kund in Rajasthan ten years later.

I was blissfully unaware of all this as I sat among naked yogis in what could have easily been the twelfth century. I was also unaware that I had already been included in the story of Hari Puri Baba. All I knew at the time was that I was about to be initiated into the Tradition of Knowledge—whatever that meant.

When the barber arrived, I knew I was in trouble. The babas all had long hair, much longer than mine. I decided that my hair was far too precious to give up without being certain that I could trust Hari Puri Baba. Maybe all these babas were just playing around with me?

"I can't go through with this, Swami Ji," I said. "I don't want my head shaved."

"You do what you like," said Hari Puri Baba, flashing his disarming smile. "But how will you become like a baby in order to obtain new knowledge? I should have him shave all your hair, down there too, not just your head and face. How will the three worlds know you are my disciple, Rampuri, if you don't follow the Path?"

I asked him what this "rampuri" business was all about. He assumed that I understood much more than I did, including that I had acquired a new name. I had been in Amloda Kund only half a day and had already lost my own name. Anyone becoming a sannyasi is given a new name, a name for entering into a new world. It was then that I discovered that Hari Puri Baba had named me Ram Puri.

He explained to me why he had given me this name. Puri is

like a last name, passed down from guru to disciple in the tradition of the sannyasi. In the fifth century BC, Adi Shankara formalized preexisting groupings of renunciates, shamans, and yogis, into an order that became known as the Order of the Ten Names, the members of which became known as Sannyasis. One of those names was Puri, and it has been passed down, guru to disciple to the present day. Ram is a common Indian name taken from the god Vishnu's incarnation as the prince from Ayodhya who rescued his princess from the demon Ravana. The name Ram was chosen by Hari Puri Baba largely on the basis of an astrological calculation. Rampuri also means a distinctive knife—a switchblade—that comes from the town of Rampur, after which it was named.

Adi Shankara, who many believe was an incarnation of Shiva, was perhaps India's greatest thinker and reformer. He renounced the world at the age of eight, having mastered the sacred books of the Vedas, and in twenty years he not only composed many of India's greatest philosophical and devotional texts, reformed the religion of the Brahmins, established India's four great centers of learning, and formed the Order of Sannyasis, but taught a way of knowing oneself that is still widely practiced around the world—Advaita Vedanta. He vanished from the world (literally) at the age of twenty-eight.

A small troop of children followed me to a shaded area in the rocks where the barber would practice his art on my scalp as I considered my options. Should I make a break for it and run? How far was it to the main road? How could I escape?

But, hold on. I wasn't a condemned man walking slowly toward the gallows clinging to his one hopeless fantasy of freedom. It was only a haircut. Drop your attachments, I said to myself.

The barber handed me a small mirror in a rusty frame so that I could watch the clumps of hair fall from my head. The children giggled as they watched him shave my beard and then my scalp with his open blade. He smiled as I felt my smooth cranium, with one short tuft of hair remaining on the top back of my head. "Guru Ji," he said, giving it a slight tug.

Hari Puri Baba had assembled four other sadhus in the ashram's *puja* room. The room was dark, and it took a few moments for my eyes to adjust. The walls were covered with rotting photos of awe-inspiring sadhus and posters of Indian gods and goddesses. Straw mats were spread on the floor, and a few sticks of incense burned on an altar housing several deities and a few small Shiva lingas. Amar Puri Baba placed a bundle in front of Hari Puri Baba consisting of an ochre *dhoti,* a coconut, a *rudraksha* seed strung on the *janeu* string of the twice born, and two strips of white cloth that serve as a lingoti. Raghunath Puri, Silverbeard, a tall sadhu with long arms, directed me to sit down facing Hari Puri Baba.

Pandit Shesh Narayan entered the room with a brazier burning with red coals from the havan between two iron tongs. The pandit, Hari Puri Baba and I formed a triangle, with the brazier in the middle, and the room started to fill with smoke.

With his eyes turned upward, the pandit intoned a river of mantra, magic syllables that flowed out of his mouth. I understood that he was invoking the great powers of the universe. At the end of each verse, each Vedic *sloka,* he would toss fragrant powders onto the glowing coals, pronouncing *"Svaha!"* consecrating the offerings in the name of the fire deity's wife.

I watched the white smoke rise from the coals, carrying the sacrifice of these sacred syllables to the gods. He dripped holy water into my right hand, then rice, flower petals, and more water, all the while intoning mantras. When he had completed the ritual, he took a small brass bowl, a *katori,* from the altar and commanded me in English to drink from it. The greenish liquid looked and smelled very strange.

"What is it?" I asked Hari Puri Baba.

"Oh, nothing much," he replied, "a substance to remove all your bodily impurities, a nectar that pleases nature."

"What's in it?" I asked.

"The five products of the cow: milk, curd, ghee, cow urine, and cow shit," he replied matter-of-factly.

"Really? And I'm supposed to drink this?" I asked, praying that he was making one of his jokes. It didn't taste as terrible as I thought it would. I imagined myself turning to gold as the liquid permeated my body. Pandit Ji turned and smiled at me as he left the room to us babas. Raghunath Puri placed the bundle in my hands.

"Now is when you ask me to make you my disciple, my *shishya*," Hari Puri Baba said.

I picked up the bundle and placed it at his feet, asking him to make me his shishya.

Raghunath Puri interrupted on a minor point. All I could understand was the word "guru."

"I am not his guru!" Hari Puri Baba shouted at him in English.

"You're not?" I was stunned. What was going on?

Pointing to the altar, Hari Puri Baba told me that, in fact, he was not becoming my guru but only my *shakshi* guru, a "witness guru" to my becoming the disciple of the lord of yogis, Guru Dattatreya, he who shows the Path. The small bronze icon of Dattatreya on the altar had three heads, those of the gods Brahma, Vishnu, and Shiva. Dattatreya is the naked one.

"It is by his grace that you enter this world of discipleship and knowledge," Hari Puri Baba said. "It's at his feet that you sit. He is your guru. I'm just doing my duty.

"He is there on the altar and also here in our circle, our little mandala, in the form of five sannyasis who walk the Path. These sannyasis will be your five gurus. I have many presents for you, and the first are your five gurus. Each will give you his own gift. My second gift will be the guru mantra, those syllables, those sounds that will anchor you to me, and through me to the Path, and act as a foundation and ultimate refuge."

Hari Puri Baba pulled the hairs on his chin and frowned. "Do you commit your life to the knowledge of God? To the knowledge of Self, the *Brahmavidya*?" he asked.

Because this was the first real vow I had taken in my life, I hesitated. What if I'm wrong? I asked myself. Maybe I shouldn't be doing this. And then I knew in my heart that either through this initiation and this guru, some other, or maybe none at all, I would always seek the Path of Knowledge. The vow I made to myself was the most important. "Yes, I do," I replied.

"Will you return to your village and abandon this guru/disciple tradition?" Hari Puri Baba asked me sternly. No, I answered him three times as he asked me three times. I knew that I could never return to my life in California.

Mangal Bharti, another of my five gurus, flung the ochre dhoti over my head. I heard a few sanctifying drops of water hit the dhoti, as the cloth was held tight by three gurus. Hari Puri Baba entered my ochre cave with knife in his hand. "Don't worry. This won't hurt a bit," he whispered, as he bent my head and sliced off the remaining hair with a rather blunt knife.

He took my shorn shining head in his hands and turned it so that the right side of my face was now facing his mouth. His breath tickled my eardrum. "Now close your eyes, concentrate, and listen very very carefully," he whispered even more quietly. Time stopped, there was utter silence, the world ceased to exist, the universe retreated into the void. And then the wind, a hot hurricane. My right eardrum exploded in flame as Hari Puri Baba's loaded breath entered it. In harmony with the ringing came the syllables, one after the other, holding onto each other, tied on a string: the guru mantra. It played way too fast, and I couldn't hear it properly. I didn't concentrate enough. The most important of mantras! How could I let my mind wander at a moment like this? Then he blew it into my left ear, and back and forth between ears, until three times it had reached each ear. As the cloth was pulled away, a chorus of

> *namah parvati pate*
> *hara hara mahadev!!*

greeted us.

> *Hail to Shiva,*
> *that Lord of the*
> *Lady of the Mountain!!*

I was sent to the spring for a quick ritual dip, and then returned to the dark puja room, where I was made to remove my loincloth and stand naked before my five gurus. "He looks like a Muslim. He's circumcised just like them!" joked the balding Mangal Bharti, slicing one index finger with the other as if it were a scalpel. Everyone laughed.

"You look so funny!" laughed Hari Puri Baba, holding his sides. "Just like a big baby! You see, nothing in your hands, nothing on your body, you have nothing. See? No more luggage! By the authority vested in me by all the mad people of the world, I declare you cleansed of all sin!"

Ramavatar Giri grunted at Hari Puri Baba, showing him two strips of white cloth. "Oh yes," he continued, "your guru, Ramavatar Giri, wishes to give you the gift of the loincloth, the lingoti." Ramavatar Giri tied one of the white cotton strips around my waist, and made me double over the other strip, sliding it over the first, then covering my genitals, before tying it around the back. Then he tightened it.

"This gift of lingoti will push your vital airs, *pranas,* upward and awaken the sleeping goddess Kundalini deep within you. It will make you strong, able to perform austerities, and sharp of intellect. It will direct your attention up, past the five elements that constitute the material world, to the spiritual world," Hari Puri Baba instructed me.

Raghunath Puri mixed white ash, called *vibhuti,* with water in a small brass bowl to make a paste. Vibhuti is no ordinary ash, but a substance of power. "Vibhuti is from the sacred fire, the *dhuni,* which never goes out. We make all our sacrifices into the dhuni, and use it as a means of exchange with the powers of nature. It has in it the fruit of countless sacrifices, and indeed is illusion burned to ash. Duality cannot stand the test of fire. The gift of vibhuti is your material wealth and your clothing. It is the ultimate medicine, it can heal, but then you can make anything you want out of it. It's primal stuff," he said. Raghunath Giri applied the thin paste to my forehead in three horizontal lines. He then handed me the bowl so that I could smear the mud of ashes like a mask over my face and body.

As he repeated a mantra, Amar Puri Baba slipped the rudraksha bead on the janeu string, over my head.

"My brother, your guru, has given you the gift of rudraksha. This bead, which as you can see, is a seed from a tree, contains the power of discipleship. It is the manifestation of the covenant between humans and the Great God Shiva that the Path of Knowledge would be passed down through the tradition of discipleship. Shiva's most uncompassionate manifestation, Rudra, shed a tear of compassion for mankind, and this became the Rudraksha tree. It pulls the pranas upward, and can be worn anywhere on the upper body to focus energy, but the one the guru gives you is worn over the heart, where your connection with the guru is established."

Mangal Bharti concluded the giving of the five gifts by wrapping me in the ochre dhoti, creating little sleeves for my arms as he folded and tied the cloth in the traditional sannyasi way. "This final gift of the five is your protection and sheltering of Mother Earth. You see, it is the color of her soil, ochre, her life-blood. You see how long this fine cloth is when unfolded? It is a flag marking that you are in her hands, and that you are on the Path."

From the waist folds of his own dhoti, Amar Puri Baba pulled a hundred-rupee note, and a rupee coin. He put the money in my hand and motioned to me that I should give it to Hari Puri Baba. I went to put it in his hand, but Amar Puri Baba grabbed my wrist, directing me to place the money under Guru Ji's foot.

"Areh wah, baccha!" Guru Ji said. "This is a large *dakshina*. Well, you are from London, or some such place, where the streets are paved with gold, no?" It mattered little that Amar Puri Baba had given me the money nor that I was as broke as any starving Indian peasant. In that moment, cash was not just money. "This is the sacred fee for the teacher. What do you call it, your tuition, no?" Hari Puri Baba said, chuckling. Holy money, I thought.

Amar Puri Baba put my hands together in an attitude of prayer.

> *om namo narayan!!*
> *om namo narayan!!*

He saluted, and I repeated,

> *om namo narayan!*

"This is the mantra we use to greet the guru, and to salute each other, *Om namo narayan!*" Guru Ji instructed me. I was then shown how to make obeisance to the gurus—*omkars*—every morning and evening to all gurus. Squatting flatfoot, with my hands on the ground, I touched my thumbs to my pinkies and learned how to count on my fingers as I repeated:

> *om guru ji! om dev ji! om datt ji!*
> *om swami ji! om alakh ji!*
> *om namo narayan!!*

Each time I made a mistake, and I made many, I was corrected. I performed five cycles to each guru, bending down, touching my forehead to my thumbs at the end of each cycle. Amar Puri Baba provided me with a rupee coin to give to each guru as dakshina.

Invoking Shiva (Lord of the Lady of the Mountain), my gurus shouted:

> *namah parvati pate*
> *hara hara mahadev!!*

Raghunath Puri Baba took the sacrificial coconut in his hands and examined it. The small, round, bearded fellow was not to have a surgical beheading. He was brutally smashed on a rock. Cleanly. One head became two skull bowls, each spilling sacred liquor. Smashed open as an offering to the gods, to mark the initiation and begin the marriage. Like smashing the wineglass at a Jewish wedding.

The coconut was full of milk. "A good sign," said Hari Puri Baba. "You will be a fruitful disciple; see how much milk there is!"

Raghunath Puri then scraped off the coconut flesh and mixed it with *gur,* natural brown sugar made from boiling and then cooling sugar cane juice, that solidifies into golden brown cakes. "The taste of the goddess Lakshmi," Hari Puri Baba said. He picked up a small chunk of gur with his fingers and put it in my mouth. I then, on cue, placed a chunk of gur in his mouth. Raghunath Puri studied me for a moment and asked, "Gur sweet, or guru sweet?" I answered, "Guru." He repeated the question twice more and each time I gave him the right answer. He lifted the *thali,* or tray, over his head and shouted three times,

> *Mahant Hari Puri Baba Ji ka chela . . .*
> *Ram Puri Ji!!*

Having made the *pukar,* the announcement to the three worlds that I had become Hari Puri Baba's disciple, and that my new name was Ram Puri, he distributed the mix of coconut and gur first to the sadhus present, then sent the thali out to the other sadhus and to the Brahmins making the havan, the fire sacrifice.

The sacrament of the five gurus, the *panch guru sanskar,* was complete, the guru-shishya relationship initiated. Now that I was his shishya, Hari Puri Baba told me that he would have me made a sannyasi at the coming Ardh Kumbh Mela in Prayag Raj, Allahabad, after *Makar Sankranti,* when Surya the Sun entered the house of Makar the Crocodile, approximately Aquarius. Until then I would need training, lots of training.

I felt very different after the initiation. I felt I could walk on air (without crashing to the ground). I knew that if I bought a lottery ticket, it would be the winning one. I stared at my shaved head in the mirror. It was naked. That's not the me I used to know, I thought. But I wasn't a new person; I just carried a little less baggage.

I had made a solemn vow before holy men. That night before sleeping I sat for a while at the spring, surrounded by the gods and prayed that I might be worthy of my intentions. My bare head felt cold, unprotected from the elements.

om purnamadah purnamidam

purnat purnamudacyate
purnasya purnamadaya
purnameva vasisyate
om shanti shanti shantih !

That is whole, this is whole.
From the whole, the whole is manifested.
When the whole is taken out of the whole,
The whole still remains!

5

"I Can Only Show You a Path"

Well before sunrise the next morning I was roughly shaken out of my sleep. The dark room rumbled with a chorus of snoring, like waves crashing on the beach. Amar Puri Baba's impatient face slowly came into focus. "Let's go," he said.

I struggled to get my bearings. There were a number of bodies sleeping on the floor, and on one of the two *charpais,* country beds consisting of a wooden frame supporting a thick net made of hemp rope, was someone I assumed was Hari Puri Baba, covered with a shawl. My head was cold and the first stubble made my scalp feel like fine sandpaper. Yesterday had not been a dream.

Go where? For God's sake, it's the middle of the night! Amar Puri Baba hurried me out of the room, saying *"Yam-niyam,"* but it was too early for me to understand anything. He sensed this and, raising his voice, repeated, *"Yam,"* which sounded to me like "yum," and I thought he was suggesting that this was supposed to be fun. He, however, had been referring to the first limb of yoga, *yam*— discipline.

I hadn't been given even a day to think about discipleship. At

3:40 a.m., after brushing my teeth with a twig from the *neem* tree, I was sent off to the "jungle" to perform my toilet duties.

Onetwothree
Allindiafree!

This was the first duty: the body must be disciplined. I had no idea how to shit on command, but I went through the motions (unsuccessfully) and rejoined Amar Puri Baba just down the hill. He made me wash my hands thoroughly with vibhuti ashes and water. Ashes, the pure. Soap, the polluted. I watched how he jumped into the tank of the well and enjoyed a quick but thorough bath, but he made me squat on the ground, and very slowly poured *lota*-cup by lota-cup of water over my head. Boot camp had begun, and Amar Puri Baba was my drill sergeant.

Wet and shaking with cold, dressed in my loincloth lingoti, I followed Amar Puri Baba to pick flowers and offer some of them to a linga, Shiva's phallus, and to Hanuman, the monkey god. When we arrived at the sacred fire, the dhuni, Amar Puri Baba's two still uninitiated disciples, Sham and Sundar, decorated the open hearth with the rest of the flowers. They also put some on the half a dozen six-foot iron tridents dug into one corner of the dhuni. Amar Puri Baba squatted in front of the fire, removed a pinch of vibhuti with his right hand, and holding it between his thumb and his ring finger, intoned an unintelligible mantra, threw the ash into his mouth, and applied the remainder to his third eye. He retreated a foot, crossed his hands on the earth three times, and performed his omkars the way I had been instructed the previous day. I remembered Hari Puri Baba telling me to perform my omkars twice a day to all gurus. This was my cue, and I copied exactly what Amar Puri Baba had done. Dhuni is also guru.

Womb of vibhuti, the dhuni is a person, a deity, a power, a god! The Mother of Fire, as Wind is the Father. A spark, the light that makes the darkness of ignorance disappear as if it never existed. A dhuni is the sacred fire that glows (*dhu*) as the Sun shines (*dhup*). It burns the world to ashes, and from those fertile ashes, that carbon molecule, another world manifests itself. Vibhuti, the ashes, heals, serves, attires, and creates prosperity. Amar Puri Baba showed me how to cover my still wet body with vibhuti, which made the cold vanish.

Amar Puri Baba placed incense inside the fire pit and then dug into the ashes with the chimpta, the dhuni's iron tongs, to expose the sleeping orange coals. He gently placed a couple of dried cow dung patties on the coals to revive the fire and within a couple minutes there was smoke. The dhuni had awakened.

Sham handed his Guru Ji frankincense and other tree resins, ghee, sesame seeds, and finally some milk, all of which Amar Puri Baba offered to the deity, dhuni. Both of the boys signaled to me, pointing at Amar Puri Baba's feet with their eyes, and I bent down and performed my omkars to my rudraksh guru.

He extracted a tin from under the mat he was sitting on and put some ganja in my hand, showing me how to rub it, then added a few drops of water to bring out the resins. The sun hadn't yet risen; the jungle around us was gradually rustling with sounds and movement. I lighted his chillam, as he mumbled mantras under his breath. The sweet smoke of the cow dung mixed with tobacco and ganja and this attracted the other sadhus to the dhuni, who were also completing their morning duties. *"Om Namo Narayan"* was exchanged as a greeting among all present. The company was assembled except for Hari Puri Baba.

As Surya the Sun started rising, as the first of his steeds approached the horizon, I saw that the festival of the day before had vanished as if it had never happened. Everyone had departed, some to their local villages, some to Chaumun and other towns, and others to Jaipur and further. The Brahmins had taken the night train back to Ujjain. This diaspora included three of my five gurus and their disciples. They all crammed into Arjun Singh's Willys Jeep. Duty complete, time to go.

Hari Puri Baba was a late riser. "Was it a rejuvenating sleep?" asked Amar Puri Baba derisively, who had been up for three-and-a half hours as a well-groomed Hari Puri Baba sat down next to him on the raised ground at the head of the dhuni. "The best ever," chirped Hari Puri Baba. Amar Puri Baba glanced at me bringing my attention to Hari Puri Baba's feet. More morning omkars. "I travel at night," Hari Puri Baba said to me as I squatted in front of him, touched his feet, and began my liturgy,

om Guru Ji, om dev ji, om . . . .

"By airmail." He turned to Amar Puri Baba as I continued my omkars, "You are a *tapasvi,* a baba of severe austerities, so you need your three hours of sleep. But me, I have work to do at night, guru bhai," he said. "I don't need any sleep!" Amar Puri Baba retorted. "Ah, but you are a blind devotee," Hari Puri Baba continued as I completed my omkars and touched my forehead to his feet. He gave me a tap where my brain connects to my spinal cord. "And what are you, a Muslim fakir?" asked Amar Puri Baba. Everyone laughed.

A joker and sometimes comedian, Hari Puri Baba would have fun with some of the most sacred traditions and idioms of the *Sanatan Dharma,* what is often called Hinduism today. He would play devil's advocate, constantly challenging his own tradition. A blasphemer in any other religion, a true believer in his own.

"Remember, Ram Puri, do as the guru *says,* not as he *does!*"

Amar Puri Baba frowned as he instructed me, skillfully ending the sparring with one of his very rare victories over Hari Puri Baba. Hari Puri Baba, however, enjoyed seeing his guru-bhai win.

gururbrahma gururvishnu
guru devo maheshwara
guruh sakshat parambrahma
tasmai shri gurave namah!

dhyana mulam gurormurtih
pujamulam guroh padam
mantramulam gurorvakyam
mokshamulam guroh kripa!

Amar Puri Baba chanted.

Guru is Brahma, Vishnu, and Shiva.
Guru is Supreme Knowledge manifest.
I offer my salutations to that guru.

The root of meditation is the body of guru.
The root of puja is the feet of the guru.
The root of mantra is the speech of the guru, and
The root of Liberation is the guru's grace.

I was proud to be appointed keeper of the dhuni by Hari Puri Baba. This meant that my place was at the dhuni. I was its constant companion: I slept there, ate there, and repeated my mantras there, "maintaining the glow from which the smoke rises." I adjusted the logs, added a new one when necessary, and offered anything I ate or drank to the dhuni first. Whenever I wasn't engaged in other work, I sat next to the sacred fire. Not just anywhere but west by northwest, at the right side of Hari Puri Baba's *asan,* his seat. And, as dhuni keeper, I wore just a loincloth and vibhuti, the sacred ash. At night, I was allowed only my thin ochre dhoti as a cover.

Like a river, a dhuni is always changing. Each dhuni also has its own personality that is as much subject to moods as people. The glow of the dhuni is both a receiver and a transmitter, and like a screen on which Rorschach-like images are projected, it delivers code. Late at night I would have visions as I stared into the fire and let my eyes go out of focus. At first I saw tridents and conches, flaming spears and a lotus, snakes and bulls, and then one night I saw a yellow-eyed, fat-bellied man riding a ram. Hari Puri Baba informed me that I had been very fortunate to have the darshan of Agni, the God of Fire.

I came to know the dhuni intimately, knowing just what pleases it and what does not; what makes it smoke and fume; and what makes it flame up, glow, and display its blue plumes; how to put it to bed at night, burying a large thick dried cow patty deep in its ashes, so that its sleep is secure; how to wake it in the morning also with a dried cow patty, but this time the thin brittle kind, broken up into small pieces; and what and how much it likes for its meals.

The dhuni also develops loyalty. As a dog usually barks at strangers, the dhuni blows smoke in their faces. No matter where a newcomer may choose to sit, regardless of the direction of the wind, the smoke will always blow in his face. The dhuni and its smoke play and dance in the subtle winds, its brothers, unperceivable by humans, unless displayed by the dhuni's wisps of smoke and its glow. No matter how great the mastery a baba may have over his dhuni, the dhuni remains aloof when it comes to strangers. I recall a number of friends who have visited me over the years at Kumbh Melas who had to endure the rude behavior of my dhunis.

One early morning, Amar Puri Baba made me commit to memory a twenty-eight-syllable string, which I remember to this day. It is the Path of Yoga and its complete description. It is not a mantra but a *sutra*, an esoteric language that conveys a great body of knowledge in a very few syllables. This *Yoga Sutra* enumerates eight simultaneous steps, which were given to us by Patanjali, that Rishi-Sage, master of yoga, grammar, and compression, to whom the elimination of a syllable was equivalent to the birth of a son, more than two millennia before zipping and unzipping files became the rage among cyber *walas*.

The eight "limbs" of Patanjali's Yoga Sutra are:

1. There exists *yam,* which is control.
2. There exists *niyam,* which is prescription.
3. There exists *asan,* sitting.
4. There exists *pranayam,* control of the breathing.
5. There exists *pratyahar,* withdrawing from identification with what our senses perceive.
6. There exists *dharan,* retaining steadfastness of mind.
7. There exists *dhyan,* focusing, meditation.
8. There exists *samadhi,* integration of the above seven into a union called *Yoga.*

Later that day, I got up the courage to ask Hari Puri Baba for a routine, for a yogic practice, a sadhana.

"Sit with your back straight and don't let your mind wander," he said, "It's that simple. That's all I can tell you. For the rest, ask Amar Puri Baba."

"So, first, you break all tradition and make a foreigner a disciple, and now you want *me* to be his Guru Ji?" Amar Puri Baba scowled.

"You already are his Guru Ji, guru bhai, you forgot, already?

Giving rudraksha? Make baba another chillam!" Hari Puri Baba
said raising his eyebrows.

"Don't remind me," said Amar Puri Baba.

Hari Puri Baba turned to me.

chitta vritti nirodhah!

He chanted. "Yoga is stopping the chatter of the mind," he said,
"Worry about the little things, first, the little world you are to
renounce."

He removed from his neck a rudraksha mala, a rosary of a hundred and eight seeds, and placed it around mine. "I suggest you sit
every morning after your bath and do *japa*, repetition, of your guru
mantra—fifty-one malas a day," he said, and turned on his transistor
radio to listen to the news amidst great static on All India Radio.

I did find a routine, but it was not the yoga sadhana I expected.
I washed dishes, greasy pots, and clothes, cut vegetables and helped
in the kitchen, and swept the dhuni and several of the rooms. Amar
Puri Baba made sure I wasn't idle. Twice a week I would accompany
him or one of the other sadhus to Chaumun for supplies. I barely
had time to do my japa of guru mantra in the very early morning.
During the day, I would sit at a right angle to Hari Puri Baba's right
side, a step below him, on the ground at the dhuni while he held
court.

I fancied myself a yogi when I sat for long hours at the dhuni, late
at night, and in the very early hours of the dawn. I saw myself wearing
ashes, keeping my back straight, and naked save my lingoti, counting
mantras on a rudraksha mala in front of Shiva's sacred fire. I imagined myself on top of the Himalaya, in Shiva's Mount Kailash, practicing austerities. I would practice a few yoga asanas I had learned in
the States after I had done my guru mantras. I imagined Kundalini,

a mysterious force sleeping in the base of the spine, rising, and awakening all my chakras. I had read all about this before ever leaving America. I dreamed about the ancient books of the Hindus, not the Vedas or Upanishads, but the ancient secret teachings. I wanted to know about my past lives, and astral travel . . .

I told Hari Puri Baba about these musings. He said he knew lots of ancient secret books, but none of them had any pages. He laughed. "We memorize everything, son," he said, "Even if they had pages, how would you understand them?"

"I'll learn Sanskrit," I offered.

"But then all you can know is the words," he said.

"But there is meaning in words," I said.

"Meaning is the sound," he said.

The babas at Amloda Kund always greeted each other with the expression *Om namo narayan*. I asked Hari Puri Baba its meaning.

"Ah," said Hari Puri Baba, "you want translation, meaning, or its power? They are three different things, you know. Its power lies in its six syllables, *na, ma, na, ra, ya, na*. When you are able to form each syllable, making its sound, you will have its power. Don't worry; you will get it. If you want English words to substitute, think of it like this. *Na-ma* is your name but what is your name? How are you known? What is your reputation? So *na-ma* is the power of respect, a salute. *Na ra ya na* is that god who gives humanity to man, and that god rests in the heart of man, as he rests on his great serpent in the ocean of milk. He is this lord, this *Vishnu*."

"But is it *nama narayan'* or *namo narayan*? I thought you and Baba Ji said *namo*," I asked.

"There is mimicking the way a baby does, there is hearing what you think you hear, and then there is picking a sound, a precise vibration, and receiving . . . more than hearing. So, *na-ma* is really *na-mah* or even *na-mas*, but when it joins with *Narayan*, it becomes *na-mo.* To maintain order in the world, sound must change as it joins with other sound, vibration must change when it joins with other vibration," he explained. "But you must discover meaning for yourself. I can only show you the path. That is my duty. Then you must walk. The tradition is not to be found in books. Okay, you can purchase the books of Adi Shankara, but even if you can understand what he says in Sanskrit, you will discover that he says that without the commentary of the tradition—interpretation by a teacher in the lineage—the sound of the guru's voice is missing, and the written words on their own have no meaning. By themselves, books, ancient or modern, are useless."

I felt a sharp pain in my left foot, as Amar Puri Baba whacked it with the iron tongs. I had allowed it to face the dhuni, which is taboo. Respect for the dhuni, like respect for other people, means not pointing your feet in its direction. Amar Puri Baba demonstrated how to touch the ground and my earlobes for my lack of good manners, and I learned that it is inauspicious for other people to see lack of respect demonstrated.

"You are Brahman," Hari Puri Baba said to me. "What is Brahman? Dhuni is also guru. Look here. See the glow, the Fire? Brahman is the great Fire. The universe is filled with Fire.

"See, the rain god is this Fire. And the logs in the dhuni, they are the mark of time, the year. You see how the year is burned up? The smoke rising from the dhuni is the clouds. When the dhuni flames, this is lightning, and crackling sparks are thunder. The gods offer *soma,* nectar, into this fire and from this sacrifice comes the rain.

"Now see this world as Fire, no different from this Fire in front of you. The logs are the Earth. The smoke is the night, and the sparks, the stars. The gods offer rain into this Fire. From this sacrifice comes food.

"Now see man is this Fire. The logs are his open mouth. The smoke is prana, his life breath, the flames are his tongue, his speech, and the sparks are his eyes. The gods offer food into this Fire. From this sacrifice comes semen.

"Now see woman as Fire. The logs are her womb. The smoke is her hair, the flame is her genitals, the embers are the act of love, and the sparks are pleasure. The gods offer semen into this sacred Fire. From this sacrifice comes the human.

"The human lives his life, and when he dies, he is offered to the Fire. Thus, all is Fire, the Great Fire, Brahman," concluded Hari Puri Baba.

The initial zeal with which I approached the life of an initiate slackened as the months passed. The novelty of wearing vibhuti wore thin as I started noticing how dry my skin had become. "Service to the guru" became "chores," which I sought ways to avoid. I dreamed of dishwashing liquids advertised on TV as I tried to remove the grease on iron pots with ashes and cold water. And what about a hot shower? I tried to remember what that experience was like. But these thoughts were distractions. What I really wanted to do was practice yoga, the real yoga, and except for my late night and early morning mantras, which weren't quite so late or early as they had been, I watched the days pass, performing my duties and sitting at the dhuni for hours on end while Hari Puri Baba held court and I was bored. I began to wonder if this was all there was to life as an initiate.

In the ashram of my imagination, the guru sat before his many students leading them in a variety of spiritual exercises, yoga asanas, and chanting. He walked around correcting our mistakes and giving us encouragement. This was clearly never going to happen in Amloda Kund. Hari Puri Baba was a storyteller. He would sit at the dhuni, his transistor radio at his side spitting out scattered signals, and entrance his audience with tales of great sadhus and their teachings, the exploits of gods and heroes, and how the last chief minister lost his office. As my Hindi improved, so did my appreciation for his art, but still I felt there was something more he should be teaching me.

"What about yoga asanas and raising my Kundalini, Guru Ji?" I asked.

Hari Puri Baba burst out laughing. "You want that snake to eat through your brain and come out of your head?"

"Yes," I answered, calling him on his contrariness, "yes, I'd like to have that experience."

"Don't worry, you will," he said, pouring warm milk into a katori and then calling the crows. Three crows swooped in, landed next to him, and dipped their beaks into the milk.

"Shouldn't I be doing yoga asanas?" I asked him.

"It depends," he answered. "It's an interesting issue, this hatha yoga business. You are correct in your idea that if done properly, asanas can give health, strength, and longevity to the body, so it is very good, no? But suppose the entire Chinese army practiced these asanas. Would they hesitate to cross our border and slaughter our population? It would just make them more effective killers and their maintenance would be considerably less. My point is that our tradition emphasizes knowledge, and as long as you can see the world (and that means also the human body) as illusion, and understand how we create illusion, then by all means, perfect your body. But the moment you become attached to your body, you fall into the trap of *maya,* and all is lost. As I have told you before, if you keep your back straight all the time, you will be almost there."

He called Kedar Puri Baba over. Although I had spent a considerable amount of time with the small, yet aloof young sadhu, this was the first time that I realized that Kedar Puri Baba was my true guru-bhai, the other guru mantra-receiving disciple of Hari Puri.

All the young sadhus called Hari Puri Baba, Guru Ji and performed their omkars to him twice daily. They were not Baba Ji's true disciples, but they honored him as their guru. I had no reason to believe Kedar Puri Baba was any different from the rest of them. Hari Puri Baba instructed Kedar Puri Baba to teach me some yoga asanas and pranayam, regulation and control of the breath.

"I would focus on the pranayam," Hari Puri Baba advised. Later he told me that what was called *hatha yoga* today was not really part of the Naga sannyasi tradition but belonged to the Naths, a later tradition of sadhus also known as "torn-ears" (because their ears are torn to insert their large black earrings).

Each morning thereafter, Kedar Puri Baba and I would find an empty room, hidden from prying eyes, to do some asanas and pranayam but nothing fancy. Kedar Puri Baba, a sadhu since childhood, was extremely agile, and I felt clumsy in front of him.

"The akhara will never accept you, Ram Puri," he blurted out one morning. "They will never allow your *vidya sanskar,* your initiation into sannyas."

Kedar Puri Baba could be irritating and certainly had a way of rattling me. He also snored louder than any one I've ever met. "Why not?" I asked. I could feel my face burning. "Isn't it up to Guru Ji? What does the akhara have to do with this, anyway?"

"You're a foreigner. It's not allowed," he said.

"But Guru Ji said . . ." I started, as Kedar Puri Baba interrupted me.

"Guru Ji, Guru Ji! Guru Ji said . . . Ram Puri, Guru Ji says lots of things. And you understand nothing. He is trying to challenge the akhara. He should have been given the holy seat, the throne, of the great monastery at Ujjain, when his guru died. But our elders considered him too young, too, uh . . . radical. It was wrong, but still the akhara is the power."

"But what does it matter that I am a foreigner? I'm a man, flesh and bones like you, and in fact, you are my guru-brother, no?" I asked. "I thought we were above this petty differences stuff. I thought the body was an illusion."

"It does matter, Ram Puri. You would have to make peace with each of the fifty thousand Naga sannyasis of Juna Akhara, for every one has his own opinion. Juna Akhara, our akhara, is the order of all the lineages of Naga sannyasis who are in the tradition of Dattatreya."

"I don't think Guru Ji would tell me I would be initiated at the Kumbh Mela, if that wasn't going to happen," I responded angrily.

"Guru Ji is very powerful," said Kedar Puri Baba. "Let's see what he does."

6

What Is Remembered

When Hari Puri Baba and I walked over the hill to a nearby Hanuman temple, there was a lot of action as it was Tuesday, *Mangalvar,* Mars-day, Hanuman's day of the week. This is a day that is not auspicious to begin a new project or a journey, but it is good for meditation, worship, and charity.

Local villagers thronged the small temple built into the side of the mountain. They smeared sticky *laddu* candy on the closed lips of the huge *sindur*-orange Hanuman. One of his legs was anchored to the ground, but the other was lifted, giving the impression of flight. His muscular build and facial expression made me think of Superman and his alter ego Clark Kent: humble yet powerful; absentminded but devoted to the service of humanity.

They massaged his legs and other smaller icons of Hanuman with wrestler's mustard seed oil, and then emptied their small paper bindles of orange sindur powder over his head, rubbing the two into an oily pigment. This sacred coloring was placed on everyone's third eye. The temple pandit smiled proudly as he put a *bindi* dot on my temple as well, and then he attended to the ritual needs of Hanuman's many devotees.

This was not my first meeting with the burly orange monkey

god, Hanuman, as he is by far the most popular god in all of India. At this point in my life, I put monkeys in a subhuman category. I saw them as foolish and lacking human logic, without the mind that separates man from beast. Hanuman is not the king of monkeys, but the monkey god for humans, or so it seemed. Prodded by Jung, I asked myself what he symbolized.

"You see all these poor village people?" Guru Ji asked. "They come to Hanuman Ji because he is accessible to all and gives his help, his blessings and magic, to anyone who asks with a pure heart. He helps Lord Vishnu find and rescue Sita and is the redeemer of hopeless causes."

I watched how people pushed and shoved their way to the front to receive Hanuman's blessings, as if he were a real person. There seemed to be more to the statue than the stone from which it was carved. His devotees would come at the same time every week to see this stone monkey and leave with the strength to face the ordeals of their lives.

He's not a symbol at all, I thought. I studied his benign marmalade face, the laddu crumbling from his mouth, and his powerful body, and I felt an intimacy, a personal contact. I wanted very much to get to know this "person," but how do you get to know a deity?

"You must understand that Hanuman is *Mahavir,* the great hero who searches the Three Worlds for the greatest treasure, discovers it within his own heart, and brings it back to his people. Let me tell you a story about Hanuman so that you can begin to understand a little about the Path.

"Now," he continued, because all Indian storytelling begins with "now," "Vayu, the God of Winds, he who carries sound and the breath, the pranas, the father of Agni, the God of Fire, was in the mood for love. He roamed about, sometimes as a breeze and sometimes a hurricane, when his passion boiled over. One day,

Vayu was blowing purple mists over the green hills of the mountain Mandara, when he spied an *apsara,* a heavenly nymph, cursed by her lord, *Brhaspati*-Jupiter, to take a birth as a monkey-girl. This monkey-girl, known as Anjana, could assume any form, and when alone in the mountains, she reverted to a beauty unequaled among mortals. Unfortunately, despite a very amorous life with her monkey husband, she had no children.

"Vayu was enchanted and circling her invisibly, he blew away her garments, embraced her, and impregnated her. Anjana cried out in shame, demanding to know who had violated her. Vayu whispered first in one ear then in the other that he meant her no harm, but had entered her with his thought. He told her that she would bear a son, whose powers would have no limit.

"Hanuman was born to Anjana in a nearby cave, and his birth freed her from Brhaspati-Jupiter's curse, so that she was able to leave the world and her monkey child and live in the *devalok,* the world of the gods, in her apsara-nymph form."

The unthinkableness of Hari Puri Baba's story tickled me. Planets cursing heavenly nymphs in the world of gods! A thought phallus! Hari Puri Baba had narrated the story as if he were talking of the neighbors or his cousin Charlie. His intimacy with divine beings made the world and my problems seem insignificant. I asked him where he had gotten these stories.

"From my gurus," he said. "It is What Is Remembered. Shall I continue?" he asked. I nodded sheepishly.

"This monkey Hanuman was born with a monstrous appetite. Before Anjana departed, she blessed him and told him to eat fruits 'as ripe as the rising sun,' pointing to Surya the Sun. As soon as his mother was gone, he looked around the cave for something to eat but there was nothing. Outside the rising sun was as red as a ripe orange. He had misunderstood his mother's words and thought that breakfast awaited him on the horizon. He leapt into the sky, flying at the speed of the wind, his arms reaching for the fruit." Hari Puri Baba chuckled.

"This happened to be the day of a solar eclipse. Surya had ventured into the cruel demon planet Rahu's realm. Rahu, who causes eclipses, is only a bodiless head. He was about to swallow Surya and cause an eclipse, when he saw little Hanuman racing toward the Sun. Something was very wrong, so Rahu quickly summoned Indra, chief of the gods.

"Rahu appeared even bigger and juicier than Surya, and with eyes like full moons, Hanuman started to pursue him. Rahu managed to escape, but then Hanuman threatened Airavata, the elephant mount of Lord Indra himself. To restrain him, Indra fired his *vajra,* his divine thunderbolt, which struck the monkey on the jaw and sent him falling back to earth.

"Vayu tried in vain to revive his unconscious child and eventually took him to the Patala region, the underworld. When Vayu left the world, sojourning 'south,' as it is said, the earth started to suffocate because there was no wind. Even the breath in all living things began to vanish. Prana withdrew to its master and fire now dominated the Earth. So all the major gods and goddesses came down to Patala Lok, their hands folded reverently, their heads bowed. Through their combined power, they revived the dazed monkey-boy, who sustained a permanently swollen jaw. *Hanu* means jaw. The gods and goddesses begged Vayu to return, and blessed his son, Hanuman, by bestowing on him all their powers," Hari Puri Baba continued.

"Doesn't that make Hanuman, God?" I asked. "If he has all the powers of the gods and goddesses?"

"Having power and using it are two different things," he replied. "And knowing the illusion of power is a third thing. I have all those powers as well!"

"Really?" I asked, not really sure if we were talking about the extraordinary world or the world of hard science.

"You have those powers too. Everyone was given those powers when Hanuman received that blessing. Every time Hanuman is given that boon, we are given those powers," he said.

"It happened several times?" I asked.

"It happens." Hari Puri Baba said cryptically, with emphasis on the present tense. "And remember, the infant monkey Hanuman, sired by the Wind, already so powerful that he almost ate the Sun, now has powers that far exceed even this. And he is naturally mischievous, as most children are. His mother lives on another planet, and his father is blown away, blinded by his pride for his son. Hanuman likes to play with power. He especially likes to tease the rishi-sages living in the jungle close by. He steals and hides their ritual implements for the Vedic sacrifices. He holds his belly, barely able to control his laughter as he watches them search for the stolen items.

"One day as he swings in the trees near the ashram of the rishi Trnabindu, Hanuman catches hold of a ferocious tiger and a bull elephant, and ties their tails to the gateposts of the rishi's ashram. When Trnabindu emerges for his morning constitutional, the shock of the tiger trying to attack him and the elephant trumpeting causes his heart to stop for a moment. His shock turns to righteous anger, and the heavens roll with thunder. The last thing one ever wants to experience is the anger of a rishi. Through his yogic powers, he perceives that the culprit is Hanuman, and he summons him to face his punishment.

"Because Hanuman so abuses his divine powers, which even a great rishi can't take away, Trnabindu curses him." Hari Puri Baba said, his voice becoming grave.

"Now listen carefully, Ram Puri. This is very important: The rishi's curse makes Hanuman forget his powers until such time as a member of his own species reminds him of them by asking for his help in the great cause! Hanuman would no longer be his true self until the moment arrived to serve the world as only he could do."

This started to make sense to me but what was this great cause? Saving the world? What was there to save? The world is illusion, injustice, and hypocrisy. That's what makes it the world. Perhaps the great cause was the path of the hero itself? He who remembers who he is, no longer bound by ideas of past and future, the witness who finds the sacred treasure within himself, brings it back to his tribe, and in so doing saves the world, again and again?

"That's right!" said Hari Puri Baba. "Time is merely an illusory stage on which the theater of repetition is performed.

"Now," the master storyteller continued, "Lord Ram was searching for his kidnapped princess, Sita. Ram had helped Sugriv, the king of the monkeys, recover his kingdom, and in return Sugriv commanded all the monkeys in his kingdom (including Hanuman) to help find Ram's abducted and beloved Sita. Four search parties were established, one for each direction. Ram knew that Sita would have been taken south, so he asked Hanuman to go with that expedition.

"Before he set off, Ram called Hanuman into the cave where he and his brother Lakshman would be waiting. Ram shocked Hanuman by telling him that he knew who Hanuman really was, even though Hanuman himself didn't know, and he told Hanuman that he trusted him, and indeed loved him more than any of the other monkeys.

"He presented Hanuman with his signet ring, explaining that there was no difference between him and his ring, and that once he had found Sita, he was to show her the ring, and she would know without a doubt that Hanuman was truly Ram's representative.

"After numerous adventures, Hanuman and his troupe of monkeys reached the Southern Sea, as far south as they could go, and a vulture told them that Sita was being held prisoner on the island of Lanka. Jambavan, the bear, one of Hanuman's gurus, reminded Hanuman of his true but hidden self by calling upon him to serve the great cause. Awakened at last, Hanuman grew to a height of a hundred feet, and clutching Ram's ring to his heart, he leaped right across the Southern Sea.

"But somehow Hanuman must have relaxed for a moment or was distracted because somehow he dropped the ring into the ocean and it disappeared from view.

Knowing that the fate of the world depended on it, Hanuman dived to the bottom to look for it. He was able to hold his breath for infinite periods of time (after all, he was the son of the Wind), but he couldn't find the ring. Eventually he came to a cave that led him to an underworld beneath the sea. Here he found a kingdom of palaces and temples. One temple that shone like the rising sun captured his attention, and he explored its labyrinthine tunnels until he arrived at a secret chamber, where a baba was chanting the name of Ram. To Hanuman's surprise, the baba called him by name, inviting him inside for a chat.

"When Hanuman started to explain the purpose of his visit, the baba told him that he knew that he had come for the ring. Amazed and delighted, Hanuman asked for it so that he could continue with his mission. The baba pointed to a pile of rings and said, 'Take your pick.'

"'I'm afraid you don't understand,' said Hanuman, 'I need Ram's real signet ring, the one that is Ram himself, the one that Sita will recognize.'

"The baba laughed. 'They are all the real thing,' he said. 'Each one is the original!' Hanuman scratched his chin and raised his eyebrows. 'Each time the age of *Treta,* the Third Age, comes around, Ram is an incarnation, an avatar, of Vishnu and you are his greatest devotee. Each time you fly over the Southern Sea with his ring, you drop it! Don't ask me why because I don't know why, but you *do.* So, you see, all these rings are his. Take your pick. When Sita sees the ring, she will rejoice. After all, who but the Mother of the World will recognize Ram's signet ring?'

"Hanuman selected one of the rings and, touching the feet of the baba, rose to the surface of the sea, and continued his journey," Hari Puri Baba concluded.

O, the names of the gods! There are hundreds of millions of them. Brahma Vishnu Shiva Hanuman Ram Sita Indra Vayu Agni Ganga Yamuna Saraswati Vishwanath Bholenath Kedarnath Bhairon Mahakal Mahakali. How will I ever know even all their names, which are their epithets and describe their personalities? Then there are the names of all the *rishis, asuras, gandharvas, apsaras, yakshas,* and *yogis,* and the names of all things and their order.

"Pronounce them!" Hari Puri Baba commanded. "The mere articulation of the names of the gods brings prosperity to Earth and blessings to the speaker. Don't say them under your breath but loudly and clearly. Invoke them. And sing, if you can, the streams of stories that all empty into story ocean. That is what brings their power to the now, here!"

The rains arrived on schedule that year, turning the oppressive dry heat of Rajasthan to steam. There were no distractions, and while Amar Puri Baba disciplined me, Hari Puri Baba enchanted me with his stories and explanations of the universe. The line separating mythology and this Extraordinary World in which I was now living became blurred and, increasingly, I couldn't see it at all.

Hanuman the monkey god, Dattatreya the three-headed lord of yogis, and Shiva, the auspicious one whose deep state of meditation is Consciousness itself, all jumped off the yellowed pages of books and sat among us. Realizing that language was at the epicenter of my new world, I spent as much time as I could learning Hindi. Slowly, I was becoming a baba.

The unremitting rain and then the hot autumn sun nurtured Amar Puri Baba's ganja plants to a height of fourteen feet before he harvested them. This put him in a jovial mood, but he didn't ease up on me. Hari Puri Baba assured me that it was for my own good, that discipline, Yam/Niyam, would give me the freedom for Asan, sitting—anywhere, with any one, at any time. But Amar Puri Baba suggested that it was also for my protection, as I would face many obstacles on the path.

The autumn also brought back the army of crows. *Kala kaka* everywhere always. They were attracted to Hari Puri Baba and perched close to him, behaving themselves. He fed them *prasad,* offerings, which they also stole, as is their nature. He used to make these funny little noises to them, and to my surprise they seemed to respond. I realized that Hari Puri Baba, sounding like an old 33-rpm phonograph record played at 78 rpm, was actually speaking to them and the crows were talking back. "Their world moves much faster than ours," he told me, "so does their language." Many babas used to know the language of birds, but now there are not so many. Why crows? I wondered. "I, like Shiva, attract marginal beings, outsiders," said Hari Puri Baba. "Crows can be great allies. And, but don't tell anyone, their language, among bird languages, is the easiest to learn."

I was having enough problems with Hindi that even the idea of learning nonhuman languages was daunting. Perhaps Hari Puri Baba made a point of speaking with birds just to push me along in my basic language skills. He also spoke less English, trying to wean me onto Hindi. "Every time I speak English to you, I make your path that much more difficult. The language of the tradition is Hindi."

Except for the few English-speaking non-sadhus who showed up at the ashram, my only English conversations were with Hari Puri Baba. He told me that he wouldn't be around forever, that his time in this body was limited. He warned me that after he was free of his mortal body, "English finished! Ding-dong, Queen Victoria is dead! Learn Hindi and Sanskrit, baccha! Without those allies, you might as well go back home, and if you are lucky, Daddy has a business you can join! Do you think you will be able to meet all the challenges of the Kumbh Mela and the akhara speaking English?"

"What challenges?" I asked, concerned.

"Too many to be named, but you will be tested," he said.

"Kedar Puri Baba told me I'll never get my initiation," I blurted out.

"Kedar Puri Baba is a fool who shoots his mouth off too much. I told you I will make you a baba, and that I'll do. The akhara cannot defeat me. If you are a hero, then nothing can stop you. Remember that gold is purified by means of Fire."

The full moon was often celebrated in Amloda Kund with great fanfare. The Kartik Purnima or the autumnal harvest full moon was no exception. Local farmers filled the ashram grounds and honored the sannyasi-yogis, including a dozen guest sannyasis, with religious songs until sunrise. This was no church choir, but Meena tribals in trance, intoxicated on cannabis, thumping out their rhythms on primitive drums, chanting their devotional hymns to the background of a harmonium that was missing two keys.

It wasn't possible to sleep, and about 2:00 a.m., I wandered down the hill to the great banyan tree, which resembled a primeval yogi, his massive dreadlocks, jatas, merging into the earth. Silver moonlight filtered down through its wide bonnet of broad leaves, gently swaying in the breeze. Several deities, including Hanuman, painted with orange sindur, were housed on a platform at its base, and they too moved in the wind. That the tree itself was worshipped was apparent from the numerous red strings and cloth tied around its great trunk and lower branches, and the offerings of flowers and trinkets at its roots. I brought incense, which I lit, and placed between some stones.

"How old are you, great banyan?" I asked the tree out loud.

"Ah, you think the tree is a person?"

I jumped and turned around. Hari Puri's moustache spread his face into a smile.

"You are correct," he said. He must have followed me down the hill. I was embarrassed that he caught me talking to a tree. I looked down and touched his feet.

"He may be a thousand years old, and just imagine what he has witnessed, and how he has defined this tiny geography, the shade he has offered for countless hot summers, the shelter for so many monsoons, the homes for animals, birds, insects, and the peace and consolation for humans. How many generations have known this banyan tree and approached him and asked for blessings, for sons, for help, and . . . for knowledge."

"Does a spirit live in the tree, Baba Ji? "I asked.

"Do ants live in an anthill? Do humans have a soul?" he asked rhetorically. "Yes, I think you could say that something without body clings to the seemingly motionless body of the tree. Okay, lets call it a spirit," he conceded. "Something that's around much longer than a human body.

"And these spirits, as you call them, need humans to perform material tasks, whatever they may be, and humans go to spirit for immaterial tasks such as the acquisition of knowledge and the blessings this may bring. The more humans believe in and honor spirit, the more that spirit manifests and speaks through humans. Have you seen the River Ganga? Is the Ganga water? Yes, humans do tend to perceive the goddess's form as water but only because we perceive gross forms of the elements. When we sing *bhajans,* hymns to the gods and goddesses, we are inviting their spirit into us so that we may know them and in that way receive their knowledge.

"You have sought out the spirit of Baba, and you have found a tap of this spirit in me. Why? Because you want the knowledge of Baba, and you now must give your corporeality over to that spirit. And that spirit clings, like the banyan spirit, to the totality of all babas and yogis, now and for all time."

That spirit of baba also found a home in Adi Shankara. As an articulator of the knowledge of the Self, he is unequalled up to the present day. When he wasn't composing his great texts and commentaries or establishing the four great monasteries, *maths,* in the four corners of India, or rediscovering countless sacred groves and shrines, he debated his way through India, overwhelming his opponents with the authority of fire, and thus revived the eternal Sanatan Dharma, the Way. His defeated foes became his disciples, and the number of his followers grew with every step.

Adi Shankara faced one final test before his Victory of the Four Directions could be proclaimed to the three worlds. He had to win a debate with Madana Mishra, and it was said that the gods themselves would come to hear Madana Mishra and even they would learn a thing or two. He was revered as the most learned man in India.

When Adi Shankara arrived, he agreed, as his unsuccessful predecessors had done, that the confrontation would take place suspended in the air, three feet above the ground. After all, one had to have qualifications. Mishra's wife, Bharati, presided over the debate, but surrendered authority to two garlands of marigolds. At the end, the man wearing the garland that was still as fresh as the day the flowers were picked, would be declared the winner.

After eighteen days of heated debate during which the open air theater of the sky was filled with all the celestial beings, the garland around Madana Mishra's neck wilted and dried out, and Bharati had no choice but to declare her husband's defeat. However, she refused to declare Adi Shankara the winner, as his victory was, as yet, incomplete. She reasoned that because she was her husband's partner in all things including his learning, Adi Shankara, even though he might be the master of all knowledge, had to defeat her also.

Adi Shankara reluctantly agreed. Bharati chose the art and knowledge of lovemaking as the final subject of debate, which was a very clever choice as Shankara was a lifelong celibate and had never experienced sex. Lovemaking was one of the sixty-four traditional branches of learning and Bharati asked him to explain the various forms and expressions of love, the nature of sexual love and its various locations in the body, the effect of the different phases of the moon on lovemaking, and how a man or woman may seduce the other. Perhaps for the first time in his life, Shankara admitted that he was unprepared and asked for thirty days in which to acquire the knowledge. This was a reasonable request and Bharati accepted.

Shankara knew that he would have to enter the body of another in order to acquire this knowledge, for knowledge was invalid without its experience. His disciples fanned out over the countryside and beyond searching for a candidate until they came upon a king on a hunting expedition who suffered a heart attack and died. This king, as kings were wont to do in those days, had over a hundred wives back at the palace, none of whom yet knew of their sire's demise.

Shankara and his disciples found a hidden cave for Shankara to perform his *kaya-pravesh,* entering of another's body, which he had learned how to do in his youth. He went into deep meditation, and one by one shut down all of his bodily functions until he, too, was no more than a corpse. Two disciples sat in the cave and protected the vulnerable body of their master, while he did his "work," for he would need to return to his own body later. He had explained to them that his vow of celibacy would remain intact because only the body acquires karma and the spirit remains a witness.

A short time later, to the great surprise and joy of his royal entourage, the king opened his eyes and sat up. Must have been only unconscious, thought his ministers and others in the hunting party as they returned to the palace. The resurrected king attended his wives, the queens, with such tenderness and passion that he was mistaken for the god of love himself. The king's body certainly knew what to do, but Shankara's spirit took it to new depths of experience and knowledge. So quick was Shankara's grasp of the art and knowledge of love that within three days of practice, he was able to compose a treatise on love that he named after the king.

His ministers suspected something. The harvest was extraordinary, the trees were heavy with fruit, cows doubled and tripled their production of milk, and peace and prosperity reigned in the kingdom as never before. They suspected that the king had indeed died, and some baba had entered the king's dead body. Body-entering was not uncommon, and the ministers wanted to take no chances on the yogi returning to his own body, thus deserting the kingdom, so they sent soldiers out to look for the lifeless body of an ascetic, and they found Shankara's body.

Fortunately, Shankara's thirty days was just about to expire, and he managed, by a reversal of his yogic power of kaya pravesh, to make it back into his own body as the soldiers began to cremate it. As the flames were about to rise, Adi Shankara jumped out of the funeral pyre, sustaining only a burn on his right hand, and thus saving his own body. When Shankara and his disciples retuned to Madana Mishra's place, Bharati conceded defeat before a word was uttered. She had already read the outcome in the stars. Madana Mishra gave away all his wealth to the poor and became a sannyasi, the disciple of Adi Shankara.

It was time to venture forth. The Kumbh Mela was still a couple of months away, but Hari Puri Baba felt that I needed to get out on the road, to practice what I had learned.

"You must toughen yourself up for the Kumbh Mela. Meet other babas, establish connections, use my name, that's what its all about. Go to holy places. Don't smoke too many chillams. Keep your back straight," he instructed.

I did need time to reflect on the preceding months before making the commitment I would have to make at the Kumbh, the commitment of renunciation.

On the day that I left Amloda Kund, Hari Puri Baba called me into his room.

"I have some gifts for your journey" he said. He gave me a shiny brass *kamandal,* a water pot, with a broad handle from Bhuj in the state of Gujarat. "For the moment you will use this to carry water, for all your needs. Later, you will fill it with *amrit,* the nectar of immortality," he instructed. Then he gave me a small woven shoulder bag with eight corners and innumerable pockets. Inside the major pocket was a mala, a rosary, consisting of one-hundred-and-eight small rudrakshas. "This *jholi* is the sannyasi's bag-of-wishes, containing in its deeper pockets, everything you will ever need. May you never have cause to use it, but if you do, what you need will be there. Practice your guru mantra on this mala, and when you have made the rudrakshas ripen by your sadhana, by your austerities, by the heat of your *tapas,* give them to your disciples. You must prepare for your hero sacrifice at the Kumbh Mela, my son," Hari Puri Baba said. "Shiva likes you. Go to his city, Kashi, Varanasi. You must go there to die."

7

Kashi

The City of Liberation

There is no city in the world as old as Kashi Puri, also referred to as Kashi, Varanasi (where the Varan and Asi rivers meet), or Banaras. Few cities in the world are as picturesque as Kashi, a city laid out on the Ganga, the river, the goddess, which has nourished the fecundity, which we now identify as the timeless North Indian culture.

Massive *ghats* step down to the river from the city in broad platforms and upon these teems the spiritual and religious life of India. The Ganga is considered so pure here that it is said to be able to expiate any sin or bad karma. The first duty of every pilgrim is therefore the *Ganga snan,* the holy bath in the Ganga.

This is Shiva's city, and people here call him Kashi Vishvanath, the Lord of the Universe. He resides in this holiest of cities in the form of his linga, his phallus, which is enshrined in a great temple.

The goddess Annapurna, the Earth Mother named as Plenty of Grains, serves Shiva with such attention and abundance that, compelled by her devotion, he remains here forever. Kashi grew from the thighs of Plenty of Grains, where the Ganga suddenly turns north, away from the ocean, so she can have darshan, behold Shiva in his primordial home on top of Mount Kailash, in what is now Tibet.

Shiva is not normally a city dweller. His untamed nature demands a remote and barren landscape, but after his marriage to the Lady of the Mountain, Parvati, he chose to dwell with his bride in Kashi.

The presence of such a trio in one place, the goddesses Ganga and Annapurna serving Baba Vishvanath, has, over the millennia, attracted babas, intellectuals, musicians, magicians, bandits, and poets, all of whom are the kind of "marginals" that form Shiva's *barat,* his entourage. For as long as people have told stories, Kashi has been not only a spiritual and religious center but a city of culture, famous for its musicians, theater, philosophers, artists, physicians, astrologers, alchemists, and its sadhus.

And then, there are those who come here to die. Kashi lies in a sacred geography where lines cross and worlds intersect. It is a holy place, a pilgrimage destination, a *tirth,* a word whose sound is generated by the verbal root *tr,* which, not unlike the Latin prefix, *trans,* means "to cross" and implies a meeting of worlds. A *tirth* is a transcendental location, where one may "cross over." Here, the rules of an Extraordinary World apply: There is a direct, nonstop flight to Liberation from Kashi. Only for the dead. Shiva guarantees it. At least, his spokesmen (and women) do. Come here to die! Just bring enough money for cremation wood and a shroud.

Count them, the twenty-four funeral pyres burning twenty-four hours a day. Enough wood, logs piled high, to build a city.

Ram nam satya hai!

they shout, shouldering the corpse. In Kashi, upon death, the human soul is believed to rise in a straight line to heaven like the smoke from incense when the air is still. In other places, the wind of one's karma, one's words and deeds, disperses the soul, as the slightest breeze disperses smoke. In other places, one attains Liberation by other means. This is Shiva's covenant with man.

Even though he is pure consciousness, Shiva does get angry from time to time. Once, the Creator God, the five-headed Brahma, caught Shiva on a bad day and insulted him. Shiva's anger jumped out of his body as the wrathful deity known as Bhairon and sliced off the haughty Brahma's fifth head. Although the violence subdued the creator's ego, it also meant that Bhairon had murdered a Brahmin. Brahma's severed skull stuck to his hand, and as penance he wandered throughout the three worlds using the skull as his begging bowl.

He finally reached Kashi, and when he bathed in the sacred waters, the skull fell from his hand and he was liberated from his sin. Shiva put Bhairon in charge of the divine administration of Kashi. Having committed the greatest of sins, he acquired an appetite for them, and was nicknamed Sin-Eater. He feasts on the sins of pilgrims seeking liberation in Kashi. In order to keep track of the fattest, the most juicy and succulent of sins, he notes down in the akashic records the deeds of all those who come to Kashi. When people die, he is there beside them, to review their deeds, and then he consumes all their sins. After this brief yet painful moment of punishment, the candidates for liberation are ready for Shiva to whisper the *taraka mantra,* the crossing-over mantra, in their ears, after which there is no return.

Yama, the God of Death, is banned from Kashi by Shiva so that he cannot carry off the souls of the dead. So why doesn't everyone come here to die? Bhairon, also known as Club-Bearer, also eliminates the unworthy. He relies on the services of his two greatest devotees: Doubt and Confusion. One must get past these two gatekeepers to obtain supreme liberation.

I walked upstream from Manikaran Ghat, past its malodorous smoke, to a peaceful bathing ghat, where I took my first dip in the Ganga, quite willing to believe that I, too, was now cleansed of sin. Why not, I thought. Anything is possible in the Extraordinary World.

I asked a sadhu bathing nearby for directions to Juna Akhara. He looked at me as if I had arrived from the moon. "Where do you think you are? You are standing on Barha Hanuman Ghat, and that is Juna Akhara!" he said pointing at the area's most prominent edifice, the grand monastery overlooking the river. This was the headquarters of the Order of Naga Babas, the Naked Ones, the Yogis. Not a place for instruction, which happens in ashrams, but a place of debate and strategy, and perhaps more important, free room and board for Nagas.

A young sadhu with dreadlocks to his waist, raced down the massive steps of the ghat with the grace of a monkey to inform me, "Baba is calling you." I saw the huge sadhu, Bam Baba, waving his arms, and I immediately recognized him from Amloda Kund. He yelled out in his booming voice, "Hey, Angrez!"

Bam Baba, one of the Naked Ones I had met in Rajasthan, had arrived in Kashi several weeks before me. He told me that Hari Puri Baba had informed him of my arrival. "He did?" I asked incredulously. "Soul telegram," he winked at me and laughed.

He refused to stay inside the akhara's monastery. "This is how Nagas live," he told me, "by the dhuni!" For Bam Baba, anything short of sleeping under the stars was prison. He needed complete freedom. I moved in with him for a few weeks, on the bank of the Ganga, just beneath the akhara. We had a tent, but that was for protection from Surya, the Sun's piercing rays during the day.

He was a true tapasvi, a renunciate in the most extreme sense, and many would come to receive his blessings. He hadn't a care in the world, and his only possessions were what he could carry on his back. He was *digambar,* literally, "clad (only) in the (four) directions." He had no income, yet never lacked anything. It was as if there were invisible servants consistently catering to his needs.

Baba Ram Nath Aghori also had invisible servants. One day he called all the local babas for a feast, a *bhandara,* he would prepare on Dashashwamedh Ghat, a half-mile downstream from us. Even though the local shopkeepers and others laughed at him when he announced that he would feed his guests from the meager resources of his humble dhuni, just a couple of small pots, hundreds of babas arrived.

The babas sat in a *pangat,* two pairs of long lines each facing another. Plates made of leaves sewn together with twigs, *patals,* were placed in front of them. They were served the traditional bhandara lunch of vegetables, dal, puris, and halwa, and of course, a one-rupee note as dakshina. Everyone was amazed that Ram Nath Aghori was able to feed so many people with such small pots. The pots had no bottom.

After the meal, he announced that his work was not yet finished. He had another hundred leaf plates laid out, and food served (but without dakshina). A large crowd gathered to touch his feet, but when he started barking like a dog, they all recoiled. Then, from every street and alleyway, an army of dogs raced to the ghat and devoured their prasad.

Then he had them lay out another hundred plates of food, this time with the one-rupee-note dakshina. "Ladies and gentlemen!" he announced. "This round is for my friends, the spirits and the ghosts!" and immediately, all the food and money vanished.

One day Uncle Bam Baba said, "Do you think your Guru Ji gave you that kamandal only to use for the toilet? That's what you think, isn't it?"

Indeed, that was one of the major functions of my brass water pot with a handle. Traditional India still uses water instead of toilet paper, which is considered unsanitary. When we crossed the Ganga every morning in a rowboat to what we called the "jungle" and disappeared behind the bushes for our morning duties, we carried our water in our kamandals. We would meet on the river beach, where we would bathe and scrub our polluted kamandals with river clay until they shone brightly and were pure once more. We would then fill them with the sacred water of the Ganga. Like a soldier's polished rifle, the kamandal must always be ready for action, and never unloaded. Someone might ask for a drink of water. Whatever comes from a baba must be pure.

"For debased humans the kamandal is just a water pot," said Bam Baba, "but in the hands of the physician of the gods, Dhanwantari, it is the container of amrit." I wanted to make sure I knew what Bam Baba meant, so I looked up the word in my *Universal Hindi Teacher* and confirmed that it meant "ambrosia."

"Not any ol' juice," continued Bam Baba, "but the nectar of immortality! That's the real reason you are taking your kamandal to the Kumbh Mela. After all, *kumbh* is a jug and *kamandal* is a kind of *kumbh*. You must fill it with amrit."

"And how will I find this amrit?" I asked.

"You have come to Kashi to find death, isn't it?" he asked. "And you will go to Allahabad to find 'no death.'"

This was a little confusing, but I realized that he was defining *amrit* for me. *Mrit* means "death," and *a-mrit* means "no death," as the vowel "*a*" negates what it precedes.

"Now," he said, "before time was counted, the gods and demons decided to forget their differences for a timeless moment, and joined together to churn the Ocean of Milk for that treasure of all treasures, the nectar of immortality, amrit. Why?" he asked.

He answered his own question. "Because the gods lacked the numbers and strength to do this on their own, so they invited the demons to become partners in the greatest enterprise the universe had ever witnessed."

"Live forever!" he shouted and his massive body shook the earth. "Defy and defeat death," he said more softly. Three babas strolling along the river came running over to the dhuni when they heard him roar. Bam Baba told them to sit down and listen, and put a pot of tea on the fire.

"The gods and the demons agreed that they would share the amrit and any other treasure they might find in the very sea where Vishnu dreamt the world into existence while sleeping on the coils of his endless serpent.

"They turned Mount Meru, the axis of the world, upside down to use as their churning rod, Vishnu morphed into his avatar, the Cosmic Tortoise who floated in the bottomless waters as a churning base, and his endless serpent stretched as the churning rope in the hands of the gods and demons. They stood on opposite shores and churned the waters as a farmer might churn fresh milk for butter.

"After a thousand years of churning, treasures started rising to the surface. The Wish-Granting Cow was first and quickly spirited away by the gods. Then came the Sea Goddess, the fragrant Wish-Granting Tree, and the Apsaras (the celestial dancers); Shiva caught Soma the Moon, which he displayed in his dreadlocks, and the cannabis plant, as they appeared; Vishnu acquired the ruby called Kaustubha, and placed it on his chest like a medal.

"Then Mahalakshmi, the Earth Mother, the Goddess of Prosperity, rose from the depths of the waters seated on a magnificent lotus, holding a water lily in her hand. The four immortal elephants, that support the Earth, filled golden pitchers from the Ganga and other sacred streams, and anointed the goddess. She ran over to her beloved, the God Vishnu, and sat on his lap. The demons were not pleased that the gods seemed to take all the booty.

"The waters bubbled and foamed. Dhanvantari, Lord of Healing, Herbs, and Longevity, holding a kamandal in his right hand, appeared standing on the water. They all knew he had *It*, the Nectar of Immortality, amrit.

"But the demons snatched it away and prepared for a fight. Vishnu [not normally known as a cross-dresser] manifested himself as Mohini, the Seductress, a voluptuous celestial damsel so beautiful that both gods and demons became enchanted. When Mohini winked her kohl-painted eyes deep as the Ocean of Milk itself, and let her upper garments fall to reveal her golden breasts, the demons were overcome with lust. She played the demons into handing her the kumbh of amrit. After all what is immortality when compared to the possibility of a moment with the goddess Mohini?

"She made the gods and the demons sit in two long lines facing each other. She was going to distribute it to the gods first and then the demons. However, the demon Rahu was impatient and managed to quaff a drop of the amrit by sitting incognito in the gods' line. As if none of the gods would notice a new god.

"Soma the Moon and Surya the Sun both realized the ruse and called to Vishnu. Angered by the cheap trick, Vishnu threw his divine discus, the Sudarshan Chakra, at Rahu, severing the demon's now immortal head, which flew off into the heavens, and the war began.

"Mohini entrusted the kumbh of amrit to the son of Indra who transformed himself into a sparrow and flew into the sky chased by all the demons. The pursuit lasted the equivalent of twelve human years, during which Jupiter guided and protected Jayant from the attacks of the demons, the Moon helped prevent the amrit from spilling (as he also controls the tides), the Sun protected the kumbh from breaking, and Saturn prevented Jayant from drinking all the amrit himself. However, during all this excitement, four drops fell to earth and landed at what is now Prayag (Allahabad), Hardwar, Ujjain, and Nasik.

"Every twelve years, which is how long it takes for Jupiter to circle the Sun, when Jupiter, the Sun, and the Moon are in the same places in the sky as they were when each drop was spilled, the amrit, this Nectar of Immortality appears, and there is a great celebration called the Kumbh Mela in each of those four places."

Mela means fair. It is the largest religious event in the world, the greatest gathering of human beings on Earth, and it is nurtured by a single drop of the Nectar of Immortality.

I examined my kamandal. At least I've found my grail, I thought. I just have to fill it up with the right stuff.

"Dis money, dis good. Dis no money, dis no good," Sohan Giri said to me from behind, emptying his entire warehouse of English vocabulary in one shot. I turned around. The baba from Thanakpur, on the border of Nepal, wore an army olive-green trenchcoat and nothing underneath. He sat down next to me at Bam Baba's dhuni and continued his discourse in Hindi.

"When you white people first came, you were rich, important, and powerful. You were sahibs and governors and viceroys, even," he said. "Now look at you. You are begging from beggars, you don't wear shoes, and you sleep on the ghat! What happened?" He crinkled his nose in feigned disgust.

I explained to him that "they" came to conquer you and rule you, but "we people" have come to learn from you.

"So before you came to take our land and our wealth, and now you come to take our knowledge!" he commented logically. "And what will you give for the knowledge? Or you just take it and run away?" he said and laughed.

It turned out that Sohan Giri was poking fun at me. He had never been serious for more than a minute in his entire life. "Take it, take it all," he said, "we give it all to you with love!"

Although this was just a joke, which the other young sadhus around the dhuni were enjoying, I had to admit that he was right. I just walk in, and because I'm a white boy, and logic and experience dictate that probably there is *some* money *somewhere,* the streets of Am-rika are paved with gold (or at least gold-plated), and because of my privilege, I presume that ten thousand years of secret knowledge should simply be handed over to me just for the asking.

After a few chillams, I walked over to Manikaran Ghat to watch bodies burn. The acrid smell of barbecued human flesh. People going to heaven. Here, the transitory nature of existence is in your face. Here no one has any rights, there is no discussion, only continuous change. When Death rides in on his mule, carrying a noose in his hands . . . who will challenge Him?

I've got to do something, I thought. Even if it's just a small step in the right direction. Like a ritual, a puja. I removed a small drawstring pouch from my bag-of-wishes, in which I kept my treasury. I counted my money, all my money in the world. Ninety-two rupees and sixty-five paisa. It's got to go, I kept thinking. It's all got to go! Why? This is the last string connecting me to the ordinary world. I no longer want to be an outsider, an exploiter, a pillager of knowledge.

The most common vows are fasts, made not for health but as marks of devotion and austerity: on Monday for Shiva, on Tuesday for Hanuman. Then there are vows to remain standing or keep one arm raised in the air for twelve years, or the vow of silence. Each person has a reason for making a vow, and usually they ask for something from the gods in return.

I also wanted assistance from the gods. I was grateful to have found Hari Puri Baba and believed that he not only possessed the ancient knowledge but also would give it to me. Still, I wasn't sure that I deserved what was being so generously given. I felt that I needed to make an offering in return.

It was about dakshina. How could I pay my fees? Could I be so lucky as to pay just on the physical level, in money? Could I *buy* it . . . for six dollars and seventy-five cents? Even if it was my last? Insh'Allah! Little did I know.

I walked slowly down to Dashashwamedh Ghat. Beggars' faces contorted in disbelief as the shoeless ochre-clothed white boy, probably quite out of his mind, handed out five- and ten-rupee notes as if they were five- and ten-paisa coins. Did he even know the difference? Lepers and widows made an extra five or ten rupees that day as I took a vow and emptied my pockets. Afterward, an old woman came up to me with her walking stick and her tin cup. She rattled a couple of five paisa coins inside. Sorry, money finished. I looked in my magic jholi for anything I might have missed and found my passport. It's also an attachment, no? The woman walked away, sensing a dry well. Thank gods, a little sense came into my immature brain at the time, and I decided not to jettison my passport.

But I did make a vow: I would not touch money. For how long? Who knows? At least a few months, until the end of the Kumbh. I will walk to Allahabad. I will eat only what is offered to me. I gave up all but my most necessary possessions, a blanket, my kamandal, my jholi, my notebook, some cannabis, my Gita Press *Bhagavad Gita,* and my passport. I stood waist deep in the river, made the offering of my vow, renounced the world, and asked Shiva and Mother Ganga for their assistance. I left Kashi the next day before the sun rose.

8

Kumbh Mela

As Surya the Sun raced toward the celestial house of Makar the Crocodile (approximately Aquarius), which, as in Western astrology occupies thirty degrees of the ecliptic, and, in fact, had reached its cusp, Soma the Moon had entered the house of Kartak the Crab, and Brihaspati Jupiter was slowly transiting the abode of Vrishak the Scorpion, I crossed the Jhunsi Bridge over the Ganga into the sacrificial grounds of Prayag. The sky was a treasure map that marked the time and place for the appearance of amrit.

From there I saw perhaps the most awe-inspiring sight of my life. I saw countless millions of human beings assembling for this great religious fair, the Kumbh Mela at Allahabad-Prayag. In every direction armies of multicolored ants filled the chaotic tent metropolis that spread its web in the triangular dry bed between the two great rivers of North India, the Ganga and Jamuna, reaching its apex where these two join the invisible Saraswati rver. These are the most ancient sacrificial grounds on earth (so I am told). I walked down into that basin, accompanied by one hundred thousand pilgrims. The numbers and colors made me dizzy, the dust was the stuff of legends.

My first kumbh. A World Series, World Cup match, or Mardi

Gras pales in comparison. One million people spread out before my eyes. Walking, sitting on the sand, under canopies, in tents, listening to spiritual discourses, looking at babas, looking at trinkets, buying, bathing, and lost. A cool million, and the party hadn't yet begun. Like the River Ganga, the faithful and the curious continued to flow into the mela twenty-four hours a day.

As the sun was setting over this confluence of rivers called a *sangam*, I was carried by the current of people down a wide dirt path that spilled into an ocean of humanity. The activities of an entire universe took place under that ancient canopy. The sandy riverbed avenues that crisscross the mela were lined with sellers of everything from pots and pans to your fortune. Hawkers with miracle herbs, miracle stones, and miracle machines gathered gullible crowds around them. Fortune-telling birds assisted their masters offering consultation to pilgrims.

Most of the people belonged to groups: families, villages, neighborhoods, followers of religious authorities, and gangs. Everyone carried huge bundles on their backs, shoulders, and heads, consisting of bedding and supplies for several weeks. Curious eyes peered out at me from heavy loads as I walked by.

Why do they all come? Why so many of them? It is said that the potency of the confluence of these three goddess/rivers is so great that regardless of one's flaws and lack of spiritual achievement, bathing here where the blue water swirls with the white, bestows Supreme Knowledge and Liberation in this lifetime. This is true at any time but during the Kumbh Mela, multiply this times one hundred thousand and eight.

This sangam, this sacred geography of Allahabad-Prayag, which is also called Triveni, the Triple-Braided One, is also present in the human body in the form of the *ajna chakra,* the third eye, the subtle wheel of energy spinning between the eyebrows. This inner two-petaled lotus is where our Surya Nadi (corresponding to the Yamuna), the hot subtle nerve current, and our Chandra Nadi (corresponding to the Ganga), the cool subtle nerve current, meets the Sushumna (corresponding to the invisible Saraswati), the central subtle nerve current, which carries the Kundalini Shakti, cosmic energy.

The five chakras, or energy wheels, below the ajna chakra have the nature of the five elements while the ajna chakra is of a mental-intellectual nature. It is the command center, as *ajna* means command. It is the guru and the location of initiation. It is that station where Shiva and his consort Shakti (in her manifestation as Kundalini) meet, and our mental activity and its offspring, Time, begins its final dissolution into the Great Void. *Chittavritti nirodhah,* the stopping of mind fluctuations, is how the sage Patanjali defines *yoga.* In the body, the ajna chakra is the port of embarkation for the spiritual journey. On the earth, it is the sangam at Allahbad-Prayag.

But the faithful also come to see the babas, the sadhus.

This was not the full Kumbh Mela for Brihaspati Jupiter had not yet arrived in the House of Vrisha the Bull, but was still half an ecliptic away. The sacrifice at Allahabad-Prayag is so powerful, that when Brihaspati Jupiter is exactly halfway there, a Half or Ardh Kumbh Mela is observed with the full program and sanctity of a Great or Maha Kumbh Mela. It is these two celestial positions of Brihaspati Jupiter, the Guru, that call the holy men and women, and the public to the Kumbh. Otherwise, every year in Allahabad-Prayag, from the time Surya the Sun enters Makar the Crocodile's House (usually on the fourteenth of January) until the second new moon after that, a Magh Mela takes place. This is the most auspicious time to make a sacrifice in Prayag. Any sacrifice.

At least half of the people on the sand avenues were as lost as I was. Whole villages were looking for the encampment of some baba of whom no one had ever heard: a camaraderie of the blind leading the blind.

As I managed to get closer to the vortex of the mela, the camps of holy men became more elaborate, their colossal bamboo archways draped in ochre, red, and yellow cloth, and swimming in small colored lights. The whining loudspeaker systems competed with one other and with the Mela Authority's PA systems. Popular religious songs—*filmi bhajans*—sacred mantras, chanting devotees, religious discourses, and lost people announcements blended into a cacophony that is the soundtrack of the Kumbh Mela. I was a drop in an ocean, now inseparable from the crowd, pulled by its tide.

If I thought it daunting that there are a lot of gods, and that each god has many names, often a thousand and eight, and was intimidated at the thought of trying to learn them all, I was bewildered by the names of the different sects. There are Shaivas, Shaktas, Vaishnavs, Bhairagis, Nagas, Naths, Aghoris, Aughors, Udasis, Ramnamis, Danda Swamis, Kabir Panthis, and Nirmalis. There are real sadhus, and fake sadhus. There are yogis, saints, shamans, healers, tricksters, tantrics, bhaktas, magicians, beggars, and criminals. The unenlightened and the enlightened.

The seven Naga akharas are lined up on the central avenue: the Mahanirvani, Niranjani, Juna, and Anand, and the lesser Agni, Atal, and Avahan. Each has its grand gate, each its chosen deity crowning the entrance. The akharas are like large military-style camps of holy men, fakirs, shamans, yogis, and other mahatmas. Some are huge, like Juna Akhara, containing up to twenty-five thousand sadhus during the peak of the mela, others, such as Atal Akhara house hundreds.

Juna Akhara is in the epicenter of the mela and dwarfs all the other camps. The three-headed Dattatreya straddles the top of its threshold archway, which is hung with psychedelic lights. A smoky haze sits over everything, the fruit of a thousand sacred fires, one in front of each tent.

An old pilgrim asked me if this was Juna Akhara we were standing in front of. I looked up at the banner draped across the entrance and slowly read the Sanskrit syllables:

> *guru dattatreya vijayate*
> *shri panch dashnam juna akhara*

Yes, this was the right place. The sign translated into my language as:

> *Dattatreya rules!*
> *The Sacred Juna Akhara of the Ten Names.*

Then the old pilgrim asked me if I knew where he could find Shankar Baba. I shook my head. I certainly didn't know. A hoarse voice behind me told him there were many Shankar Babas. The sadhus of Juna Akhara have a reputation of being especially untamed, fierce, and aggressive, and the wild man behind us was no exception. The pilgrim looked at me through his Coke-bottle-bottom glasses, his eyes magnified to twice their size, and said "Yes, there are, there must be, but this one can grant your any wish!"

I followed three young sadhus carrying bedrolls on their heads into the akhara, under the great entrance gate. The akhara was filling up. Hundreds of ochre-clad and unclad new arrivals poured in, most appearing to know exactly where to go. Senior sadhus marched, walking stick in hand, and were followed by bands of disciples carrying the wherewithal for a month-long encampment. Everywhere feet were being touched, guru-bhais and old friends embraced. Gravel-throated sadhus called out the names of new arrivals and offered hot chai tea from their dhunis, which lined the wide promenade inside of the akhara. There were thousands of dhunis, each with a number of tall tridents, *trishuls,* the weapons of Shiva, impaled, fork up, in a bed of ashes. And behind the dhunis were the tents, and behind the tents, the labyrinthine alleyways and passageways that led to back doors.

I joined the arriving babas who were eclipsed by the thousands of pilgrims who daily flood through the akhara like a great river, for the beholding, the darshan of these babas. They do so with folded hands and lowered heads, their eyes wide with awe, wonderment, and fear. For what they see is another world, inhabited by the ancient shaman yogis of India, their matted locks intertwined with garlands of marigolds and piled high on their heads like kings' crowns. Some pilgrims throw themselves at the babas' feet, others throw coins as part of the ritual of pilgrimage, that of distributing alms. Village women holding their small children cover their faces; others, as yet childless, beg the babas for fertility-bestowing ashes. They are all given the seminal substance, vibhuti from the dhuni.

Some pilgrims preferred to watch from a distance. Most pilgrims made little distinction between the rishis of their rich storytelling traditions and the nameless faces of the yogis. Some pilgrims hoped to meet a powerful patron among these shamans; however, few had the courage to approach one. Still others came to meet their baba, a sadhu that lives outside or near their village or town, one that they visit at their *math* monastery, one that they met at a tirtha or pilgrimage place, or just wandering about on the road.

"Hey you there!" a baba yelled. I looked around. "Me?" I asked, a little bit intimidated. He called me over with a wave of his hand that was not so much an invitation as a command. "Foreigner, huh?" I was asked as I sat down. "No, not there," another baba scolded me,

"Sit over there!" Then the interrogation began. Why did they talk so fast and eat their words? I got the feeling they were doing it on purpose. When finally I told them I was here to be initiated, they all laughed. They thought I was being cute. When I told them I was the disciple of Hari Puri Baba, an old sadhu said, "Well, why didn't you say so?" And I would have, had they given me a chance.

He told me that Hari Puri Baba was close by, because this *dava*, or quarter in which we were standing was *solah marhi,* the Sixteen Lineages, which are the Puris. I was quickly realizing that despite my many months in Amloda Kund, and my time on the road, I was not prepared for this. I had indeed arrived in another world.

"Ram Puri!" I heard my name yelled out. Of course, there could have been many Ram Puris for all I knew, but the voice was familiar. I turned around to see Kedar Puri Baba standing behind me. I was never so happy to see anyone in my life. He pulled me up and embraced me. "Come, Guru Ji is waiting for you," he said.

Juna Akhara was a collection of the lineages of Guru Dattatreya even before it was organized by Adi Shankara in the sixth century BC. Encountering numerous families and lineages of ascetics, yogis, and shamans, he created an infrastructure to increase dialogue, first with his Ten Names, and then with his akhara. The Ten Names was one side of the equation and originated with Shankara, the akhara was the other and goes back to Dattatreya in the Age of Treta, said to be many thousands of years ago. Each akhara belonging to the Ten Names has its own lineage following a founder-guru. But the akhara takes on a life of its own beyond the facts.

"Oho! Look who has come to the party!" Hari Puri Baba said as I arrived and performed my omkars at his feet. Although both babas' dhunis faced each other behind the leader of the Sixteen Lineages, Shri Mahant Arjun Puri's tent, Amar Puri was to be found sharing the tiger skin adorning the raised *gaddi* behind Hari Puri's dhuni, sitting on his left. As always, they were inseparable and, as always, they were arguing. Hari Puri's chest was puffed out, which was the sign that he was expounding on a sublime point of philosophy in order to win a debate.

The microcosm of the twin dhunis mirrored the beehive activity of the akhara that in turn reflected the electricity of the mela. Devotees from Rajasthan queued up to touch the feet of the two main babas, chai and chillams were in factory-like production and consumption, vegetables were being chopped, wood stacked, and all this was being performed by the naked ghosts whom I knew from Amloda Kund. It felt like home. The noise, confusion, and incredible dust seemed to vanish into the peace of Hari Puri Baba's environment.

Hari Puri Baba squinted at me as I narrated my adventures since leaving Rajasthan. He was so much more special to me now that I had more experience on the road and could see his unique qualities. I felt that I was at the source or at least close enough to the source by being around him. This was one authority I could easily bow down to.

"Have you found out who you are?" he asked.

I told him that I knew who I was not. I was not yet a baba, but I believed that he could make me one. Hari Puri laughed. "Are you really sure this is what you want? Careful!" he warned, and then laughed again. "When I make a baba, it's hard to unmake."

He told me that my initiation into the Great Renunciation, the Virja Havan, would take place on the dark moon, about two weeks later, in a grand mass ceremony. He instructed me that my time should be spent in preparation for receiving the Sacrament of Knowledge, the *Vidya Sanskar* and that I should know who I was by that time.

Okay, I thought, *two weeks to enlightenment.* I had heard

Krishnamurti say that it takes less than a second; that time is not an element in realizing enlightenment. So two weeks should be plenty. Doesn't it take a lifetime? I wondered. Advaita, Non-dualism, is a good crutch. Time is an illusion.

"And what is this initiation?" Hari Puri began, "It is an open door that invites you to enter into story." I think he meant mythology. "Not make-believe, but story that lives the way mountains live, and the sky, the rivers, and the trees . . . story that can't be contained in a book or possessed by any one person.

"You know about the churning of the ocean that produced the amrit, the Nectar of Immortality, but here, also, there is churning." Hari Puri said, pulling back his shoulders. "What is the akhara?" he asked. "It's a churn, a machine that agitates the souls that make up the ocean of the Kumbh Mela into story! No? Is a *kumbh* not a pitcher that contains all the souls who are here? Is it not also the container of amrit? The souls who are churned here have already left the world of mortality.

"And if you enter that great hall, then you must finalize your affairs in this world, for in two weeks' time, you will perform your own funeral rites."

The daily *chakra*-circle of life remained the same, except on major bathing days, of which there were three during the course of the mela. The discipline I had received with Amar Puri was helpful for my strict routine of arising at about 3:30 a.m. so that I could be sitting at the dhuni by just after 4:00 a.m. This is a very sacred time of the day, and I secretly felt macho to be meditating then and the one offering the first chai and chillam of the day to those returning from bathing in the river.

I would shake Kedar Puri awake from where we all slept on the straw inside Hari Puri Baba's tent, and we would set off for our morning toilet and bath.

It was not only dark at that hour, but there was a ground fog that only just lacked the density of water. January in the Doab, that area encompassing the Ganga and Jamuna, is cold. And on the temporarily dry riverbed of the Ganga, not only was it very cold, but also damp, and the pea-soup fog would last until eight or nine in the morning. Wrapped in the blanket in which I shivered all night, I joined Kedar Puri at the tap, where we washed our hands, and when we reached the Ganga, we would flip for who would bathe first. We employed the buddy system for on the banks the fog was thickest, and one could easily lose one's way, or worse, one's clothes. Kedar Puri and I looked out for each other. He was my brother and ally.

The water was warm, but the air was biting cold. My inner fire would start to burn as I had darshan of the element of air, and hence touch, feeling the icy mist on my skin. Wading out eight or ten feet would take me so deep into a disorienting sightless world that reestablishing geographical context on Earth was elusive. Bathing was having darshan of the element of Water. I recited the names of the seventeen river goddesses and asked them all to join Ganga and Jamuna at that moment, so that I might have full darshan:

> O seventeen river goddesses!
> May the full volumes of your waters,
> Joined with the ocean,
> Make the world happy and auspicious!

I washed my mouth and dunked three times. I offered Water to the still-to-rise Sun, then on a Shiva linga I formed with my fingers, and finally to the four directions. May the world be prosperous!

The heat from reawakened dhunis burned away the mist in small circles, and from a distance, when we returned to the akhara, I could see the muted glow of flames. The fourth element, fire, is in the form of the dhuni. It is the light that dispels darkness and the warmth that quells everyone's shivering. I take some vibhuti, taste it, make a *tilak* on my third eye, and three lines across my forehead.

Darshan of the fifth element, ether, takes place with the production of sound. I perform my Om-kars to the dhuni.

Materializing out of the mist, shivering babas multiplied, squatting around the dhuni with their palms facing the fire. Chillams helped, and a feeling of pity for each new arrival determined new rounds. As the gurus appeared, we disciples would scramble to touch their feet and perform our omkars. Often the queue for the feet of an elderly or powerful guru could be ten sadhus deep. I would make it a point to seek out each of my five gurus each morning and evening realizing, of course, that I should wait for them to be properly dressed and ready for darshan. Hari Puri would get up quite late, at least by akhara standards.

The jokes would fly about Hari Puri and his sleeping habits, and I would smile along with the giggling sadhus, even though I didn't always understand what they were saying. They didn't bear him animosity, as is often the case in the akhara, but affection in that this was the *lila,* the theater, of this baba in his story. Little did they realize, as I later discovered, that he traveled at night without his body, sometimes covering astounding distances. A lot of leeway is given to babas who are advanced in their sadhana.

Hari Puri was concerned that I pay my dues to the akhara, to the Marhi for registration, for Guru Dattatreya, for distribution of offerings, and other matters. Kedar Puri volunteered to make the rounds with me to pay all the dues.

However close I was to Kedar Puri, with his eternally youthful face, I couldn't deny that he was the Rishi Narada, the troublemaker. Not that my frail guru-bhai had any bad intentions. Quite the contrary. It was his timing. His ears were too big, as was his mouth, and he was unable to resist gossip. It was rarely *what* he said (and I heard him make some dubious statements), but *when* he said it. He seemed to search out moments of tension to drop little firecrackers. He was a sadhu and a yogi from the time he was six years old, yet, he was also a burden that Hari Puri knowingly placed upon my shoulders.

Guru Ji would not send Kedar Puri with me on a mission of any importance, and asked Silverbeard Raghunath Puri, one of my five gurus, to accompany me instead.

The lanky Raghunath Puri was a world traveler but not a jetsetter. His world was defined not by national boundaries but by tribes and cultures, and he was driven by an insatiable curiosity for marvels and wonders. He would categorize kingdoms and great cities by saying, "People there eat dogs, cats, and insects," or "There is a fruit growing on trees with great spikes that would kill a man should it fall on his head."

I had obtained some "strike-anywhere" kitchen matches during a trip home to America. Thinking to be clever, I loudly invoked Shiva, as I ignited the match with my thumbnail to light a chillam. Raghunath Puri happened to be sitting next to me, and he studied me and my little show. Then he commented that this was nothing. Chihh! He had seen it before in the Damascus bazaar in 1936. Damascus? Yes, he had been to Mecca, Jerusalem, Beirut, and as far as Istanbul to the west and had traveled through Tibet, China, Indochina, and as far east as Shanghai—all on foot.

The marhi was cautiously welcoming, but the akhara was a little hostile. Raghunath made noises with the akhara's secretary, a grumpy old baba, and suggested that he should speed up his work a bit. It appeared that there was always a tussle. I started to see that there was not the automatic acceptance foreigners often find in India.

I completed my registrations, dues, and endowments. Hari Puri had provided Raghunath Puri with the money. Eleven rupees here and there, a few five rupees, and then a few more elevens. Then fifty-one here, and a hundred-and-one there. Every time money is given, the *karbhari*, the baba who collects and accounts for money, property, and wills, writes it down in his record book: Shri Ram Puri Ji Angrez, shishya-disciple of Shri Hari Puri Ji, Hanuman Mandir, Amloda Kunda, Rajasthan, on this eleventh day of the bright half of the *Paush* moon, in this 5,073rd year of the Kali Yuga, has given fifty-one rupees to the Sixteen Lineages of Shri Panch Dashnam Juna Akhara for the maintenance of Guru Dattatreya. This is written down for every gift, financial or otherwise, that is given to any of the institutions of the akhara by anybody, for any reason. I have seen rooms full of the records of a thousand kumbh melas!

In the language of North India, akhara means a place of wrestling. Megasthenes, Alexander the Great's ambassador to the court of Chandragupta Maurya in Patliputra in the fourth century BC, named the sadhus he saw *gymnosophists,* naked philosophers, who in ancient Greece might frequent a gymnasium. The wrestling that happens at the akhara of the Dasnami Nagas is spiritual, intellectual, and political, and its maneuvers can be lethal. Every idea, thought, action is subject to challenge, and challenge can come from the lowliest baba.

"There will be opposition to your initiation, Ram Puri," Guru Ji said, several days after my arrival.

Sangharsh hone se sona shudh ho jata hai!
Gold becomes pure through strife!

It's opposition that forms the story and spins the chakra of the Sanatan Dharma. Without opposition, you have no story to tell, and no one to become.

"I have never heard of a foreigner having his sanskar in the akhara," he continued. "Shesh Narayan in Ujjain searched the records back for hundreds of years and found nothing. We sadhus have fallen somewhat in the world's current Dark Age. Not more than most, though. Many of our lineages have filled up with non-Brahmin castes, but there are no foreigners or white people, angrez! They will say that this is no place for you, that you are a bad omen. And you *are* a bad omen."

"Then maybe I shouldn't be here," I said to Guru Ji with my hands together. My voice was just above a whisper, my face reddened, and I felt a numbing in my knees.

"*Chup!* Listen to me," he said. "It's relevant. Our days are numbered and indeed already past. Pandit Nehru ensured that in 1956 when he passed a law requiring sadhus to carry identification. We know who we are and which are the rascals but the public's protector, Pandit Ji, assumed that we were all rascals, until proven otherwise. It is our relationship with the public that is central to our dharma. The public is *purush,* humanity, and we are *prakriti,* the Earth Goddess. When that balance is upset, it is up to us to restore it, and it might take greater austerities, *tapas,* than we are capable of. Our whole practice, tradition, and powers, are for their benefit, not ours. We are renunciates. There is nothing we won't do for our devotees, nothing in the three worlds.

"So the trust must not be lost . . . but times have changed. The Angrez left, but they left behind their ways and their servants, who are now imitating their master's failed modern world. Some sadhus believe that the public will trust us less if they see white people among our ranks.

"Then there are those who believe that because you are a Westerner, you must be rich, and this arouses rivalry. Both gods and demons want to possess *Kamadhenu,* the Wish-Granting Cow!" Hari Puri paused.

I had assumed that yogis, rishis, and most of all, gods, would be beyond our ordinary human emotions such as jealousy, anger, lust, and violence. But here at the Star Wars Cantina, my categories and knowledge began to fail me. There was certainly a semblance of the Old Rules, but that's as far as it went.

"I sort of understand what you've told me, Guru Ji, but I'm not sure what to do. I just want to do my duty (whatever that is)," I blurted out.

"I'm just telling you what I see." Hari Puri looked at me compassionately. "You do your duty, but do it here. Don't wander about the akhara. Go for *arati* and omkars but forget the bhandaras, the great feasts."

The next morning around ten, Kedar Puri said, "C'mon let's go!" without saying where to. After what Guru Ji had told me, I was planning to spend the day around the dhuni, but Kedar Puri kept pulling at me, like a mosquito buzzing in your ear, won't let you sleep. "But Guru Ji said . . ." I began. "Ohhh, Guru Ji!" my guru-bhai interrupted.

The akhara is a circle divided into four quarters, determined by a system of lineages: the Sixteen Lineages consist of those with the surname Puri (Ram Puri, Hari Puri, Amar Puri, and so on), occupying the northeast corner to the right of the gateway. The Four Lineages occupy the southeast quarter, and those sadhus with the surname Giri are divided into the Thirteen Lineages, and the Fourteen Lineages, occupying respectively the Southwest and Northwest quarters, the rear half of the akhara. In the center point of the akhara is the Deity, the icon of the three-headed Dattatreya, in a makeshift bamboo temple. The tents and dhunis of the four leaders of the four quarters surround the temple. The weapons and strongbox are also kept in this central area that is called the *marhi*.

Baba Rampuri Ji at his first
Kumbh Mela, Allahabad, 1971

© Goa Gil

Baba Rampuri Ji, 2001

Baba Rampuri Ji, Ujjain Kumbh Mela, 2004

© Thomas Kelly

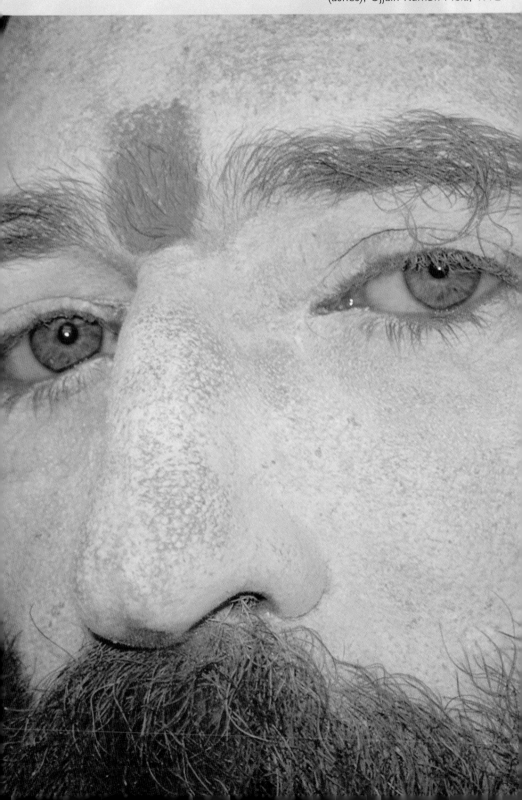

Baba Rampuri Ji in Vibhuti
(ashes), Ujjain Kumbh Mela, 1992

Datt Akhara in Ujjain, one of the
oldest cities in the world, 2007

© Goa Gil

© Goa Gil

Baba with the Pir of Datt Akhara
and Sundar Puri Ji, 2007

Baba Rampuri Ji, Kumbh
Mela, Allahabad, 2007

© Goa Gil

Baba Rampuri Ji holding court at Hari Puri Ashram, Hardwar, 2003

Baba Rampuri Ji with his siddha guru, Shri Mahant Arjun Puri Ji

Baba Rampuri Ji in his
ashram, 2006

Baba Rampuri Ji with Sundar Pu...
Ji at Hari Puri ashram, 2003

"Shri Maharaj" Santosh Giri Ji surrounded by a group of Naga Babas at Hari Puri Ashram, Hardwar, 1998

The last photograph of Raghunath Puri Ji, bidding farewell to his disciple, Adbhut Chaitanya Puri Ji, Ujjain, 1980

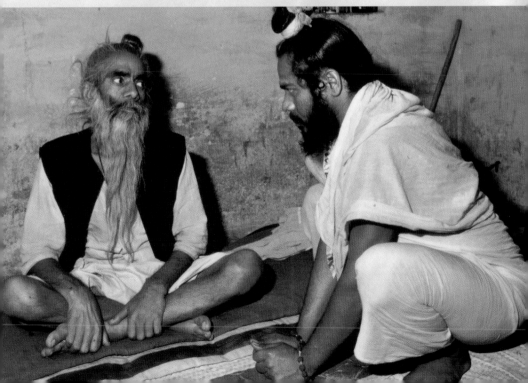

Pir Amar Puri Ji and Raghunath
Puri Ji, Kumbh Mela,
Allahabad, 1977

Kedar Puri Ji, Baba Rampuri
Ji's brother and ally, Kumbh
Mela, Allahabad, 1977

The Pir of Datt Akhara,
Shri Paramanand Puri Ji,
2007

© Goa Gil

The Mahakal Jyoti Shiva Ling (Phallus of Father
Time) adorned with *bhang* (cannabis), Ujjain

Bir Giri Ji (seated second from left) surrounded by fellow sadhus, at Shivaratri (Great Night of Shiva), Girnar, Gujarat, 1977

Baba Rampuri performs *abhishekh*, ritual bathing of the Mahakal Shiva Ling, at the Mahakal Temple during Kumbh Mela, Ujjain, 2004

Baba Rampuri Ji,
Mangalanand Ji (Goa
Gil), and Bir Giri Ji
as they return from
the sacred bath in
Hardwar, Kumbh
Mela, 1998

© Dieter Ludwig

Baba Rampuri Ji's
guru, Shri Hari Puri
Baba, a "Knower,"
circa 1969

Shri Paramanand Puri Ji, The Pir
of Datt Akhara, Ujjain

Baba Rampuri Ji with Mangalanand Ji
(Goa Gil), at the dhuni, Hardwar, 2003

Gauri Giri Ji, ninety-six-year-old Mahant from Ghaziabad, 1996

The Samadhi (death) of Siddh Giri Ji, Kumbh Mela, Allahabad, 1977

Raghunath Puri Ji (Silverbeard), 1979

Sundar Puri Ji, 2004

Pir Amar Puri Ji Maharaj, Ujjain, 1979

Pir Sandhya Puri Ji Maharaj, the grêât siddha of the 20th century, Ujjain, 1940s

Bir Giri Ji (standing) during the Shivarati festival, Girnar, Gujarat, 1977

Bir Giri Ji with coiled dreadlocks

Kalyan Puri Ji, 1977

Shankar Giri Ji, Allahabad, 2001

Rampuri Ji sits with Shri Mahant Macchendar
Puri Ji, and his guru, Shri Maharaj Kapil Puri
Ji (far right), Kumbh Mela, Hardwar, 1998

Juna Akhara is a *yantra,* a sacred enclosure that invokes and invites the deity, Dattatreya, to sit on the throne of yogis.

We walked the gauntlet of the dhunis of our Sixteen Lineages, passed the Dattatreya enclosure, and proceeded into Giri territory, heading for the dhuni of Madhu Giri Baba. I had never been to a bhandara before, although Kedar Puri insisted that it was not a bhandara but a breakfast. Although he had not been present during Hari Puri's talk the day before, he seemed to know every word that had been said. It was slowly dawning on me that everyone seemed to know everything in the akhara. The words *private* and *secret* took on a new meaning. This is one of the reasons that kings, generals, merchants, and outlaws have confided in Naga sadhus for thousands of years. Kedar Puri treated me like the kid on the playground daring you to smoke your first cigarette.

I hesitated as Kedar Puri took my hand and pulled me through the crowd of milling sadhus. This was to be Madhu Giri Baba's last kumbh after spending a hundred years as a yogi. The ancient man appeared like Shiva himself, giving blessings and *shakti-pat* as he touched the heads of those sadhus coming to honor him. His animal eyes, dark and penetrating, darted about the crowd. Once I saw him, I felt mesmerized and prayed that our eyes wouldn't meet, the way you avoid eye contact with the rowdy element in a bar. In the press I got separated from Kedar Puri and didn't see where he had gone.

A gravelly voice called my name. Oh, there are always several Ram Puris in Juna Akhara, but his voice was addressing me and coming from a young Nepali-looking sadhu sitting next to Kedar Puri, with a "hip" group of younger sadhus.

Although Bir Giri Baba looked Nepali or even Tibetan, he was from some village in the Punjab. His high Mongolian cheekbones, and especially his eyes were misleading. He nudged Kedar Puri to make room for me to sit next to him, then he called to one of Madhu Giri's disciples to bring me chai and a sweet *gulab jamun*. He also insisted that they give me my five-rupee dakshina explaining that I was the chela of Hari Puri Baba. "Give him your *parcha*, your ticket!" Kedar Puri butted in. Bir Giri laughed and exchanged the parcha that I'd been given earlier by Kedar Puri for the five-rupee note, which he slid under my knee.

Bir Giri Baba was a natural leader, a large-boned young man with a Thelonius Monk rasp and the air of a tribal shaman. He was always surrounded by a group of young fellow sadhus and there would be plenty of chillams, and someone singing filmi bhajans and banging on a small drum. At arati, the evening worship, he bugled the *nagpani,* his cobra-coiled horn, like Dizzy. The elders also gave him inordinate respect for someone only two years older than me. Later on he grew into his laughing-Buddha body, but at that time, he was still skinny.

"We meet again," he said, his face crinkling into a smile. I could understand everything he said in Hindi, and my Hindi was still rudimentary. His speech was unadorned, he had all his teeth, didn't chew pan, and didn't slur or swallow his words. His speech wasn't elegant, and his grammar followed the rules of song rather than speech. He loved rhymes and the language of story is song.

Although I hadn't actually met Bir Giri before, I had met people like him many times in my life. At a love-in in San Francisco, on the Dam Square in Amsterdam, in an artist's loft in Paris, at the Gulhane Hotel in Istanbul, and at the Bamyan Hotel in Kabul. The nationality of each one didn't matter, nor did his name, but each time I sensed an instant kinship. Bir Giri Baba welcomed me into the akhara in a way even my own guru could not, making me feel instantly as though I belonged.

I felt so much acceptance and camaraderie that day that when the following morning Kedar Puri suggested we take a stroll, I readily agreed. This time it was to the encampment of a Mahamandaleshwar of Juna Akhara, not a Naga, but an Avadhut, one chosen by the Nagas from Juna Akhara to represent them in the outside world. His encampment was outside the akhara premises. This was a full bhandara being attended by thousands of sadhus from Juna Akhara.

Inside the billowing tent, decorated with streamers and the ever-present marigolds, the Mahamandaleshwar delivered sermons to his devotees and the curious, straight lines of ochre-clad sadhus sat facing each other. Kedar found us a spot at the end of a long queue.

Have you ever had a couple of thousand naked men over for lunch in a tent encampment in a riverbed, served them individually, and then paid them for coming? Wealthy lay devotees from Gujarat cooked the feast and provided the money, but the hierarchy of the akhara makes the bhandara happen. Bringing divine order into such chaos is only the beginning of the challenge. Feasts like these are always late, sometimes by many hours. Thousands of leaf plates, *patals,* and clay cups, *kulards,* are set out in front of each sadhu. The brass cooking pots are big enough to feed them all. As is the tradition, the sadhus began to sing for their meal:

> *hara hara mahadev shambhu*
> *kashi vishvanath gange!*

Fifty young sadhus appeared from the kitchen tent with hot serving pots and ladles. A middle-aged Gujarati *baniya* got up on a stage to give a short speech and a murmur went through the crowd who was hoping that he would keep it short.

I noticed two senior babas walking in our general direction; no, they were walking straight toward us. One wore distinctive blood-red cloth, associated with tantrics.

"Get up and get out!" said the mean-looking baba in red. I thought there had been some mistake. "Tell 'em," I said to Kedar Puri Baba. He tried to say something, but the baba in red told him to shut up, with an air of finality. "You'd better go, Ram Puri," Kedar Puri told me, and before I could register my shock, two babas grabbed me by the arms, and escorted me out.

I was too embarrassed and ashamed to be angry, but I couldn't forget the faces of the two men. Then Hari Puri's voice rang in my ears, and I began to understand.

"I give you an ajna, a guru's instruction, a command to his disciple, and you ignore it? Chihhh! Do you think I say things just to listen to the sound of my own voice? Don't you credit me with any intelligence?" he scolded me.

"It's not Ram Puri's fault, Guru Ji," Kedar Puri butted in. "I took him there." Hari Puri Baba squinted at my frail guru-bhai with the incredibly bad timing before he exploded. "So it's not his fault, huh? Thank you, guru! And just who in this great web of illusion are you supposed to be? I'll tell you . . . you're a good-for-nothing wastrel! Useless fellow! Rascal! Only trouble making, I tell you!" he yelled, pulling his shoulders back. "And you, Ram Puri, this idiot Kedar Puri is your guru, or what? You follow *his* instructions? And *he* will go to the three worlds to save you?" His laughter was derisive.

I wanted a book of rules. This was all so complicated and hard to fathom. I longed for order where there seemed none. The only thing to do was to keep my mind focused and realize that I was living inside an ancient mythological text.

9

Angrez: Foreigner

My waiting ended exactly two weeks after my arrival in the akhara. The day of reckoning had come. Known as both the *Virja Havan* (the Sacrifice of Heroism), and the *Vidya Sanskar* (the Sacrament of Knowledge), the initiation into Sannyas was loudly announced by twenty-four Alekhiyas, a subsect in the akhara, covered from head to toe in holy ash. They marched from dhuni to dhuni shouting one of the names of Shiva,

alakh! alakh! alakh!

With long wool ropes wrapped around their waists and clanging their ankle bells as they shuffled their feet, they held out their bowls made from human skulls as they begged for flour.

This name of Shiva is He with No Eyes. Shiva is blind, his eyes unfocused and turned up in meditation on the Supreme Void. Look up, I heard inside my head. Abandon what lies below. The world is an illusion. Drop your attachment to the senses that perceive it. Climb to the peak of blind Shiva's mountain!

Hari Puri's eyes also went up inside his head, as he raised a chillam to the sky and taunted Shiva as he yelled:

aaaa-lakh!

kol de palak!

dekho duniya ka jhalak!

Hey You with no eyes! Open your eyes!

And see the glitter of the world!

It was customary to fast for the big initiation. This did not mean a total abstinence from food but avoiding cultivated food such as grains and vegetables. Hari Puri fed me a breakfast of yogurt and bananas before putting a piece of paper, a *parcha*, in my hand and sending me to the temple of Dattatreya to await further instructions.

At the Marhi, an itinerant red-eyed drummer whacked his dholak into a frenzy, as countless chillams circulated among the neophytes. There were old babas with white beards and wrinkled faces and preteens with not so much as peach fuzz. There was a cross-section of north Indian rural society and perhaps a few from the cities, but everyone was about to be equalized. Clad only in white loincloths we sat on the cold clay on that January morning, getting pumped up, waiting. Red caped *kotwalis,* sergeants at arms, marched back and forth, their long silver staffs over their shoulders while other Nagas would come by to inspect the new crop of sannyasis.

"Hey, Rahu!" I felt the rude jab of a wooden stick. The chatter among the disciples seemed to stop. The baba asked who was my guru in the coded jargon of the akhara, *"Prem pat kaun hai?"* (Who is your loved one?) I was prepared for this and answered his first question successfully. Then he asked to see my parcha. He examined it carefully, gave it back, and departed.

A young kotwali, whom I recognized from Raghunath Puri's dhuni, announced that we were to proceed to the sangam for our *mundan,* head-shaving, and preliminary rituals. Everyone got up and struggled to get to the head of the line because those at the front were shaved while the razors were still sharp. We marched in twos, holding the hand of our partner—whoever that turned out to be.

What I didn't know was that while I was sitting among a thousand disciples, Bhairon Puri had brought the Shri Mahant of the Puris, the ninety-year-old Arjun Puri, and his disciple Kapil Puri, as well as several others, to the dhuni of Hari Puri. Bhairon Puri, the old tantric, was furious. He complained to the group that Hari Puri's guru Sandhya Puri had accepted Muslims as devotees in Ujjain at Datt Akhara, the most sacred of Naga maths, and now Hari Puri was planning to make a circumcised foreigner a sannyasi.

Bhairon Puri could shout down almost anyone. In decibels, Hari Puri was no match for him, but he pointed out that his guru Sandhya Puri had taken back the stolen sections of Datt Akhara from the Muslims, and that, Keshav Puri Multani Baba, our marhi's *dada guru,* had made Muslim disciples. Still, Hari Puri had no ready answers in defense of a foreigner being initiated.

"How can you prevent *me* from making this boy a sannyasi?" Hari Puri asked. "I am his guru, have completed his Sacrament of the Five Gurus, and have paid his akhara fees. What more do you want?"

"He has no *gotra,* he is not an Indian!" yelled Bhairon Puri, referring to my lack of clan within the greater Indian system. "How can he even be given a janeu?" He referred to the string of the Twice Born, worn from shoulder to waist that was given as a preliminary to the sacrifice, making us Brahmins.

Bhairon Puri stormed off, leaving Hari Puri and Amar Puri sitting with the Shri Mahant Arjun Puri and Kapil Puri. "You beware, brother," Kapil Puri had said to Hari Puri. "It's just an excuse, it doesn't matter what you say, he's after you. Who do you think was the strongest voice against you in the Council of Eight? Who do you think was responsible for your failure to become Pir of Datt Akhara? Who do think props up that incompetent miser, the current Pir?"

"Get rid of the foreigner, he'll only bring us trouble," urged Arjun Puri in his raspy voice.

"And we should make the Rishi Bhrigu a liar?" questioned Hari Puri. "Who will continue my line?"

"I will give you a hundred chelas, no a thousand," offered the Shri Mahant.

"Am I so disenfranchised that I need someone else to provide my chelas?" Hari Puri asked.

Meanwhile, we marched to the confluence of the rivers and raised our arms as we shouted praises to the great God Shiva:

> *hara hara mahadev!!*
> *hara hara mahadev!!*

and heard it echoed by onlookers as they threw flowers and coins:

> *hara hara mahadev!!*

The hallowed beach had been cleared and sanctified with pots of smoking frankincense and mantras pronounced by Brahmins. Riding tall horses, the Uttar Pradesh mounted police assisted in keeping the curious away.

To my great relief, I saw Pandit Shesh Narayan leading two other pandits and the barbers. Hari Puri had told me that Shesh Narayan would be coming to perform the major rituals but was very late arriving at the mela. As he surveyed the new initiates, our eyes met. He flashed me a big smile and continued with the ancient ritual.

We had come to the most ancient place of sacrifice on the Earth, and were now instructed to find this sacred geography within our own bodies. When we reached that inner place of sacrifice, within the third eye, it became clear that we were not our bodies and that our concerns were no longer the five elements from which our five senses arise and bind us to these bodies. We were about to formally abandon this attachment, as we had abandoned our homes to enter the wandering life that led us to the Sangam. Our inner pilgrimage would proceed from the third eye to the supreme void, as on our outer pilgrimage we would walk from the Sangam to the very source of the Ganga.

The work of barbers completed, our hairless heads marked us as infants taking our final births. We were each given a rough-hewn clay cup to hold the Nectar of Immortality, and a twig, as a walking stick, the sign of the Path North. When the sun went down, we returned to the akhara. In the center, in the Marhi, surrounding the makeshift temple of Dattatreya, a sacred enclosure had been roped off and a funeral pyre was blazing in each corner.

The funerary fires were burning for us, for the initiation into Sannyas is the final sacrament, marking the end of our participation in ordinary life.

I could see that it was going to be a long night, and I managed to get a spot close to the fire. We were given mustard and sesame seeds and other fire offerings and, tossing them into the flames, I saw that the all-consuming fire of knowledge burned away the dross of ignorance.

As time passed and the logs crackled loudly like firecrackers, the loud chanting subsided into silent prayer and the monotone of mantras. I closed my eyes and repeated my guru mantra, using it as a boat to cross to the Other Side. The akhara's supreme spiritual authority, the *acharya,* started making his rounds from the far corner of the marhi, blowing mantras into the ears of each initiate, as Pandit Shesh Narayan performed the havan. Then, suddenly, two babas grabbed my arms and pulled me from my reverie.

"What's happening?" I asked. They uttered a few expletives that were beyond my limited Hindi and the word *angrez,* foreigner. I tried to resist, I called out for my new guru-bhais, I tried to explain that I had a parcha, that my guru's name was Hari Puri, that I was staying in the tent behind the Shri Mahant's, but they ignored everything I said. I was sure that it was a language issue, a simple misunderstanding. I was very wrong.

Bhairon Puri had returned to Hari Puri's dhuni and challenged him to a debate before a full meeting of the akhara, which was not so much an intellectual exercise as a show of power: vocal, physical, and tantric. He wanted a meeting convened right away.

"You want a wrestling match with me before a cheering audience?" Hari Puri asked. "What will that accomplish? I know what you want. It's a gaddi, a throne that you will never sit on. Ujjain does not belong to you but to those great ones who have relinquished their egos. It is not I that will oppose you but Dattatreya Maharaj himself!"

Those who were present claimed that they heard a small explosion, smelled foul sulfur, and saw yellow smoke coming from Bhairon Puri. His eyes were red and sweat poured off him. Raghunath Puri went over and invited him to sit down and have chai, but Bhairon Puri pushed him to the ground. Amar Puri and three others jumped to their feet. Hari Puri begged them all to calm down.

"You pull your angrez out of the sanskar now, or I will finish you," shouted the large sadhu.

"I will not pull Ram Puri out of the sanskar!" Hari Puri said, and Bhairon Puri stormed off with his two henchmen.

"Brother, you've made a big mistake," said Amar Puri. "Let Ram

Puri sit in the next sanskar in Haridwar. What's a couple of years?" he asked.

"You don't understand," said Hari Puri, "this is not about the young foreign boy. Bhairon Puri has been looking for a way to attack me ever since Gokarn Puri was made Pir. I was an easy target. However, once I did my Bhrigu Tantra, there was no turning back. If I pull him out now, we all lose everything."

"Then we had better start preparing for a battle," said Amar Puri.

"I shall do nothing. I shall not resist," said Hari Puri.

"Now, I'm afraid you don't understand," said Amar Puri. "He's not just playing around. Bhairon Puri is one of the very few living tantrics who knows how to kill."

"While some of us have spent our lives practicing austerities to remove attachments and spreading harmony and peace, this one has learned to annihilate prana, and I should prostrate before this power?" Hari Puri asked. "I shall carry on as I normally do. I shall do nothing!"

Amar Puri knew that the threat was very real, so he called a few sadhus in for consultation. He asked two of his old devotees, who were merchants from Ujjain to go out in the middle of the night and gather supplies; gold and silver plates, musk crystals, the paper-like bark of the silver birch tree, various herbs, and other magical items, so that he could foil Bhairon Baba. The *samharini kritya,* one of the most powerful of the sixty-four tantric *krityas,* can be used to kill. Amar Puri knew that once Bhairon Baba had intoned his mantra and sprinkled his offerings over his dhuni, there was no hope.

"If you are planning hocus-pocus, then count me out!" Hari Puri shouted from inside the tent.

Meanwhile I was trying to dig my heels into the cold clay, twist my wrists free from the goons who were pulling me away from the rites. The bigger one barked at me like a dog. I was being humiliated, and I was afraid that I would be beaten. Red-caped baba-cops, kotwalis, arrived on the scene, and I closed my eyes and repeated my guru mantra to myself.

As they pulled me past the boundary of the sacred enclosure, my two oppressors suddenly let go. Hari Puri and Amar Puri were standing there with Pandit Shesh Narayan. Amar Puri dressed down the manhandlers and then dismissed them, shooing the curious onlookers away with his stick.

My heart thumped in my throat when Hari Puri told me not to eat or drink anything that was given me. I asked if there was something I should know. Hari Puri assured me that everything was fine and that I should return to my funeral. He told me that Pandit Ji would soon perform my last rites.

The new initiates had formed a solid mass of flesh surrounding the pyre. I was pushed and pulled through until I was in front of the flames. I saw Pandit Ji making his way toward me, and I looked around and saw nearly everyone had his eyes closed. The smoke hovering over us seemed to be made up of the thousand souls of the Ordinary, waiting for the door to the Extraordinary to open. Or perhaps it was the vaporous ashen Shiva, giving his blessings. Shiva, Shiva, Shiva.

What was I doing? This was madness. The fire was sucking all of the oxygen out of the air. Who was the "I" who was renouncing? Who was the "I" who would receive something called a sacrament? Was I this adventurous young man from a good family in America? I was not my body or my mind, but weren't these thoughts mine? Maybe they were just flying through me, past me. Maybe I was attached to thoughts and memories, causing me to identify my self with my thoughts. My memories were a story in the present tense, creating the illusion of a past.

Even if I said to myself, "I renounce my attachment to the illusion of past and future!" I would still be stuck with the "I." I could smell the hair on my shins singeing. I could smell my body being cremated. Time moved very slowly and then stopped. I saw my life played out before me, not in the past, but in the present, and I understood that I was telling the story in the context of now. I'm ready, I thought. I am witnessing. But, I am also trying to make sense of what is happening. My rational mind determines what I witness. It picks up certain sensory impulses, puts them into categories, and then asks culturally driven questions such as what they symbolize and what the whole damn thing means. But that's not me. I'm someone else who is just watching, witnessing, staring.

The morning fog rolled in as dawn broke. I shivered and struggled to get closer to the fire that was a shadow glow of its raging glory during the night. Pandit Shesh Narayan had performed my funeral rites. I was now ritually dead. My body, my five gross elements of earth, water, air, fire, and space, was reduced to ashes that commingled with the ashes of the other initiates in the great funeral pyre.

Eyes opened as the acharya, accompanied by the sacred council, approached our pyre to whisper-blow the *Mahavakya,* also known as the supreme statement, a Vedic mantra, into our ears. This sound from the lips of this sadhu, whose human body represents Adi Shankaracharya, ends the cycle of births and deaths. Once you have heard this sound, return becomes impossible. Like the taraka mantra that Shiva himself whispers into the ears of the dying in Kashi, it is a boat that carries one across to the other side.

Towering above the other members of the sacred council was Bhairon Puri Baba. I tried to avoid his gaze, but it was impossible. Our eyes locked for only a second, but that second was enough. I knew that it was all over as he marched toward me, pushing away the sitting initiates. My body went limp, and all resistance vanished. I heard someone call my name and could barely make out Kedar Puri's face through the fog. He stood just outside the enclosure, signaling for me to get up and leave. How could I? I was so close now. I wanted to receive the mantra.

Bhairon Puri was closing in on me like Death himself, followed by his hooded henchmen sadhus. There would be no negotiation. I stood up and, trying to make myself invisible, moved toward Kedar Puri. Taking my hand, he pulled me away and said, "I told you so."

My chest tightened and tears welled up inside me. I felt small and insignificant. I wanted Kedar Puri to shut up, but he wouldn't. How could I face Guru Ji? How could I face any sadhu in the akhara? I had been humiliated, and I wanted to run away.

I touched my gurus' feet and sat down at the dhuni to get warm as Kedar Puri put a blanket over my shoulders. "You look so pitiable, child!" Hari Puri said and roared with laughter. I was so concerned with my own plight that I didn't notice how pale Hari Puri's face was, and that his back was bent. Distracted by all the laughter, I failed to see that everything was not quite right. Hari Puri sent Kedar Puri back to the sacred circle to check on the progress of the initiation, and when he returned informing Hari Puri of its completion, my heart sank even lower.

"You two idiots probably think the akhara is sacred," Hari Puri asked and looked at each of us deep in the eyes. I struggled in vain to break our eye lock. "Kedar Puri I can understand, but you Ram Puri, are you equally ignorant? The akhara is only the mundane world! Let's go!" Hari Puri commanded me, as Kedar Puri and Amar Puri helped him to his feet. Only then did I see that my guru was weak. Go where? We walked slowly back to the enclosure where the initiation had taken place and was now empty.

Hari Puri sat with his back to Dattatreya's altar, and I sat facing both Guru Ji and the deity. "In the name of the Acharya Mahamandaleshwar of Juna Akhara! In the name of the world guru Adi Shankaracharya! In the name of the guru of yogis, Guru Dattatreya! May this Mahavakya be received by my disciple, Ram Puri!" Hari Puri cried. As he had done when he made me his disciple, he took my head in his hands and whispered/blew the sacred sound, the path-affirming mantra into my ears, thrice.

It is to be heard, or *sruti,* and to be repeated as Vedic mantra. And to be translated? Well, I can't really say that with any kind of authority, but I can't help translating it for myself:

I AM BRAHMAN!

"You are free, Ram Puri. One-two-three all India free, free as the wind," Hari Puri said. "I have done my duty. The rest is up to you. You may do as you please and go where you please. Now catch up with the other initiates. They will have reached the Sangam by now. Bathing in the water there will complete your initiation."

I managed to catch up with them, dive into the waters, and bathe. I remained underwater as long as I could. I was in the womb of the Mother Ganga. I was about to be born. I was swimming in the Ocean of Milk, searching for the physician Dhanwantari, and his kamandal, his kumbh, which held the Nectar of Immortality. No, I was immersed in that amniotic amrit. Emerging from the mother of waters, I counted my first seven steps, as instructed by Pandit Shesh Narayan, with each step calling the Three Worlds and the Four Directions to witness the completion of my sanskar and my mythological birth.

The new initiates splashed water and played like children in a swimming pool for the first time, dunking each other and diving into the water. Then there was a roll of thunder, and we all looked at the sky in amazement. A large gray cloud resembling a swan appeared above our heads and dropped what looked like rain. Everyone knew, however, that it was more than rain. The invisible Saraswati River and Goddess had shown herself and blessed us with her raindrops of the Nectar of Immortality.

Excited, elated, and freezing cold, I ran back to the akhara, repeating my new mantra to keep my mind focused. Unable to conceal my joy, I rushed into Hari Puri's tent, but he had gone. I was told that he had suddenly fallen ill and departed with Amar Puri in the jeep back to Rajasthan.

10

Tantric Attack

As I stepped off the bus from Delhi at the Jaipur bus stand and started to look for the bus to Chaumun, a small man in a large Rajasthani turban came up to me and asked me if I wanted to see Baba Hari Puri. I told him that was why I was looking for the bus to Chaumun, and the man explained that Hari Puri was not at Amloda Kunda but at the SMS hospital.

When I arrived at the hospital Hari Puri appeared to be dead. He was still, his face was pallid, and his eyes were rolled up and back in his head, but I saw that he was breathing. Slow, measured breaths, so perfect that one could see no movement at all. A hushed silence enveloped him and extended as far as the next bed in the crowded tuberculosis ward in this medieval hospital. Just a few feet away one could hear incessant coughing and spitting, the clamor of the huge ward, and the traffic on the wide boulevard downstairs.

I looked at Amar Puri for a clue to the prognosis. His gloomy face made my heart sink. Hari Puri had fallen ill at the mela, so they had returned to Amloda Kunda, but by that time he was already in coma. A lay devotee, who happened to be a doctor, was there when they arrived and had Baba Ji brought straight to SMS hospital, which was the best in Jaipur.

I picked up the chart at the foot of the bed. "Name: Swami Hari Puri Ji; Son of: Pir Sandhya Puri Ji; Age: Unknown; Occupation: Saint; Complaint: Stroke." I found the name of the attending doctor, a Dr. Rathor and discovered that he made his rounds in the morning, around ten o'clock.

Amar Puri and Kalyan Puri were staying at the Jain Dharamsala across the street from the hospital. They had taken over a room in the crowded guesthouse that by good luck had a small patio, just big enough for a dhuni. The room had two beds and an altar. Amar Puri suggested I could sleep on the floor, but Kalyan Puri, the voice of reason, said that the room was too small and that I would have to sleep under one of the beds, where all their supplies were kept. I declared that if I was to sleep under anyone's bed, it should be Guru Ji's. They were impressed. I moved in under Guru Ji's bed and remained there for three months.

In 1971, in a hospital like this, the onus was on the patient's family to purchase the medicines from the many pharmacies that surround all hospitals in India, get someone to administer them, and except for the doctor's daily visit, supervise care at all times. It was the family's job to make sure that the doctor's treatment was being faithfully administered.

Amar Puri had no faith in the young Angrezi doctors, the defiling (and, according to him, useless) Angrezi medicines, the shameless nurses, or the hospital itself. Well, he did approve of the *chowkidar,* the gatekeeper, who had a fine stash of ganja, and with whom he would spend an hour each day in the guardhouse, puffing away at his chillams and telling stories of great babas. Bam Baba would have liked to help, but this was an alien world to him. I, however, came from an Extraordinary World called Angrezistan and had special knowledge. After all, my father was an Angrezi doctor. The babas were relieved that I was willing to take over responsibility for Hari Puri's medical care.

I met with Dr. Rathor, an incredibly straight young man, who couldn't believe that the son of a surgeon would be anywhere else but practicing medicine in a modern clinic in Los Angeles. Why was I here in a TB clinic, with no shoes even, trying to take care of a hopelessly ill old man? "He will never regain consciousness, and even if he does, too much of his brain and nervous system is gone" Dr. Rathor told me. He invited me to stay at his home, but I declined. Still, we met regularly, I found him to be very professional, and I grew to like him.

Amar Puri Baba was bitter and frustrated. He did not believe that Hari Puri was suffering from a stroke and was certain that Angrezi medicine wouldn't work. The only cure for Baba Ji was to offset the curse, if it was not already too late. On the patio in the ashram, he mounted his counterattack by building a special dhuni, and lit it with the fire from the Kal Bhairon Temple. He had me assist him.

I would take my bath in the hospital basement and be at Amar Puri's dhuni before the sun rose. After chai and chillam, Amar Puri would begin puja and *yagya,* the magic rituals for curing Hari Puri Baba. He would carry on all morning, but I would leave at about nine-thirty to check on Baba Ji and meet Dr. Rathor.

Before leaving, I told him that I needed money to buy medicines and the drip for Baba Ji. Amar Puri frowned but pulled a suitcase from under the bed and opened it. It was filled with bundles of rupee notes. How much did I need? A thousand? Ten thousand? I told him that a hundred would be more than enough and with that, I bought everything that Guru Ji needed.

Amar Puri was a serious baba, strict and stern, and after Hari Puri's death, he also became somewhat crabby. He was an authority on many things and was not somebody to argue with. The story is told that when he was a young sadhu, he spent years practicing austerities in the mountains, perfecting his yoga. At one point he had moved to a cave in the hills near Amarkantak, the source of the Narmada River, in what is now Madhya Pradesh. One morning, some local tribespeople came upon his cave. One of the women was very ill and could no longer walk. Her husband thought she was dying, and was trying to get her to the closest doctor who was thirty-six kilometers away. He asked Amar Puri if they might spend the night there. Amar Puri was not fond of company, and he definitely didn't want a woman in his cave, but he took pity on her.

He recited a mantra, and with his large iron chimpta, gave her vibhuti from his dhuni. Within ten minutes, all her strength returned and she showed no sign of illness. The tribals threw themselves at Baba Ji's feet, and he gave them all vibhuti, his blessings, and sent them on their way. "Thank gods! " he muttered under his breath when they were gone, and he went back to his practice.

Once the town folk heard about the baba who performed healing miracles, they started coming for darshan. They brought fruits, grains, and vegetables as offerings for Amar Puri, and he would give them his vibhuti. Occasionally he would take the pulses of an ill person, and give some of the herbs he collected or *bhasma* ash that he prepared from herbs, metal, and stones. Within a year, his fame had spread far and wide, as did the mythology of his powers. He became distraught because he no longer had the solitude he needed, and he decided to leave.

In the middle of the night, however, he was awakened to see five men with knives who demanded gold. The young men roughed up Baba Ji to make him talk, but he wouldn't or couldn't talk about any gold because there wasn't any. One of the stories that had been making the rounds about Amar Puri was that he was an alchemist, which wasn't entirely untrue. But as the story grew, it was said that

Amar Puri could make gold from iron, and that he was making the stuff right there in his cave.

When the robbers couldn't find anything yellow and shining, they sliced poor Amar Puri with their knives, took everything, and left him for dead. Eventually he regained consciousness, picked up the pieces of his body, and walked the thirty-six kilometers into town holding his intestines in his hands. A local doctor shoved everything back where it belonged, and sewed him up, without sterile conditions, anesthetics, or antibiotics. Amar Puri was lodged in a nearby ashram where he recovered from his ordeal. It is said that within one year, even the scars were gone. And within two years, each of his assailants died in a bizarre accident.

But the scars didn't disappear. He moved them from the outside to the inside, and he stopped laughing. He still had a sense of humor, but the deep belly laughs he had been known for disappeared, as did the smile wrinkles at the corner of his eyes.

We had a very formal relationship. I addressed him as Guru Ji, kept my back straight in his presence, and paid close attention to sadhu etiquette. I definitely touched his feet more often than necessary. He would badger me about my feet being in the wrong place or a spot on my dhoti, and generally acted like a drill sergeant. If I had my bath at four in the morning and started my practice at four-thirty, he would tell me to have my bath at three-thirty. I was definitely a barbarian to him.

My Bible was *The Universal Hindi Teacher*, a book owned by every foreigner in India who was even 10 percent serious. At first, I studied it, but then I would use it for reference or just pick a page. One day I looked in my bag for the book, and it had vanished. How I could have misplaced it was beyond me. It was not as if I had a lot of possessions. I could only assume that some spirit had removed the book believing that I did not need it anymore.

The mystery was solved a couple of days later. Sadhus, especially those on the road, don't have desk drawers. Yet there are those things that don't belong in your jholi-bag-of-wishes that goes with you wherever you go and those go under your thin roll-up mattress. Amar Puri Baba kept a vast inventory of necessities under his mattress, and that is where I saw my book when he went to get his stash of ganja.

As I tried to grasp what was going on, I finally understood that he was frustrated with my lack of Hindi, so he had stolen my book in order to learn English. The next day, I stole the book back from under his mattress. Over the next few weeks, we stole the book back and forth from each other and Amar Puri didn't learn any English, but we did establish the basis for a deep and rich friendship.

He did learn one English word, but don't ask me how. One morning, I decided to clean out my jholi. I sat opposite Amar Puri and emptied it all out. He reached into the pile and pulled out a very small square of paper. "LSD! " he said, proud of his English. I was stunned. I had forgotten that I had these two blotters of LSD someone had given me. He looked at me, smiled, and asked if he could eat it. I said, "Sure, what is mine is yours, Guru Ji, as you know! " I thought he was kidding, but he wasn't. He ate it.

He wanted to know what was going to happen. I told him that it would make him a little crazy, that he would feel and see things differently. Perhaps I should have prepared him better. It was ten o'clock, and I had to meet Dr. Rathor, so I told Amar Puri that I'd be back to check on him. He told me not to worry.

I forgot all about Amar Puri and his acid trip, as one thing led to another in the hospital, and hours flew by. Then suddenly it hit me, and I dropped everything to run over to the *dharamsala*. But I didn't have to go far before I encountered Amar Puri, in the middle of one of the busiest streets in Jaipur, trucks and cars whizzing by him, bicycles and scooters, buses and cycle rickshaws, all beeping their horns and ringing their bells, and shouting. He was turning around in circles in the middle of the street. I grabbed him by his trembling hand and led him back to the dharamsala.

Several days after his acid trip, Amar Puri told me that he now understood why I had to leave the land of my birth to come to India. He also told me that I could assist him with the repetition of the sacred *Mahamrtyunjaya* mantra. "Supreme Victory Over Death" is how I translated the name of the mantra that is also a name of Shiva. He explained that the mantra was Shiva himself and that there was no more powerful mantra for healing. Perhaps if I joined him in a forty-day japa, we could bring Hari Puri back. When he told me that he would teach me the mantra and how to use it, I was overjoyed. Mantras such as this one were among the treasures I was seeking.

11

The Healing Mantra

The following Monday, the day of Shiva, which falls on every Monday, my instruction began in a mantra that could save Hari Puri Baba's life. I showed up half an hour early as Amar Puri instructed, so we would have time for puja, yajna, our rituals and meditation, and perhaps a chillam or two, before the mantra *diksha*. A *diksha* is a little initiation, a *showing the way*. We sat opposite each other. Amar Puri closed his eyes and hummed mantras until he was out of breath, then took another deep breath and continued. Finally, he grasped my head, and blew the mantra into each ear.

Then Amar Puri smiled and told me that he had planted the mantra inside me. Now I needed to nurture it by first memorizing the syllables. He sounded each syllable, and I repeated it after him, but his smile faded as I continued to make mistakes. I wanted to write it down, but he wouldn't allow it. Not that it shouldn't be written or even published, for it is an elixir of life for all humanity, but I understood that this was not "book" knowledge, even if it was my own notebook. He persisted with his oral transmission, and eventually I managed to get it right.

Dr. Rathor shook his head despairingly when I asked him what I could do to help Hari Puri. "Okay, massage his fingers and toes, if you need to keep yourself occupied," he said. I repeated the mantra silently while I worked on my baba, although I was afraid that this wasn't its appropriate use. The Higher Powers will understand, I thought.

On the following morning, Amar Puri repeated the ritual and blew additional seed mantras into my ears. He explained to me that the more the mantra is repeated, the more it unfolds. There are elements in the mantra such as compression and mnemonics that self-extract. It's not a question of interpretation, but one of use. It's not what a mantra means, but what it does. Least important of all is translation, which is always without context and is ahistorical. Critical to the use of the mantra is an articulation coupled with a particular mental association, neither of which I yet possessed. I would have to go deeper into the tradition of sound to taste the nectar of the mantra and for its fruit to be known.

During the night of Mahashivaratri, the once-a-year sacred night of Shiva, which marked the end of the post-Kumbh Mela period in Kashi, Amar Puri took me on a cycle rickshaw for a tour of many of the Shiva temples in Jaipur. We had consumed an overgenerous amount of *bhang,* edible cannabis, grown in Amloda Kund. We brought with us *bael* leaves and *datura* seedpods for the Shiva lingas, a large bag of coins to distribute to the beggars, and hashish, as sacred gifts for the numerous sadhus we encountered. We stayed out until the sun rose.

As I tried to squeeze life into Baba Ji's toes, other babas started filing into the hospital room with lowered heads and folded hands. Silverbeard Raghunath Puri Baba and the tall, one-toothed Darshan Giri Baba were the first to arrive. Raghunath Puri brought some special ayurvedic tonic from Kashi, prepared by the legendary Tripurari Trivedi. It was bhasma, ash, distributed among a dozen paper bindles, to be taken once a day. Raghunath Puri dropped the bindles into my open hand as I looked at him hopelessly. Not because I thought it was too late and he was going to die, but because I couldn't imagine injecting ashes into Hari Puri Baba's drip. Mangal Bharti Baba arrived with his chelas, then Kapil Puri Baba, Kashi Puri Baba, Ravi Puri Baba, and even Lakshman Puri Baba. The tuberculosis ward metamorphosed into a temple, for not only were there now at least a half dozen, well-appointed, powerful sadhus, but the patients on the ward and their families would come for their darshan and vibhuti. The hospital cooks also became devotees and provided us with a constant supply of hot chai. And, of course, the chillams. I guess chillam-smoking in a tuberculosis ward is no more a contradiction than sadhus from the fifth century BC camping in an Angrezi hospital.

With the arrivals also came news that Madhu Giri Baba had left his body on the penultimate day of the mela. There had been a grand procession starting from his dhuni, where his corpse had been tied to a wooden frame so that he continued to sit as he had sat there during his life. Covered with vibhuti and marigolds, with his mala in his right hand, he was carried to the Sangam. Crowds threw flowers and coins at him, and drummers announced his coming and going. He was stuffed into a burlap sack, which was then weighted with heavy stones. The boatman rowed out to where the white water mixes with the blue in a downward swirl and Madhu Giri's journey ended when his body was thrown into the water where the Ganga meets the Jamuna with a cry:

> *om namah parvati pate*
> *hara hara maha-aa dev!*

Even though several of the babas were my gurus, and many others I had met and had come to know at the Kumbh Mela, the time they spent at SMS hospital brought us closer together and enabled them so see me in a different and favorable light. All the sadhus saw me as his chela, performing his service, his seva, which is more defining of the guru-disciple relationship than all the teachings. Initiations are necessary, but only seva seals the bond. No matter how hard I had tried in Amloda Kund, I had been unable to serve him like the others. Amar Puri and I continued our morning sessions and now were joined by an overflowing crowd of yogis.

Hari Puri refused to die. So, all but three sadhus departed and that left five of us, the minimum required to carry his corpse to its final resting place.

Exactly forty days after we began the Mahamrtyunjaya mantra, while I massaged Hari Puri's fingers, his eyes opened. He looked at me blankly, as though he were trying to focus, and his lips quivered, but no sound came out. Again he tried, and I can still hear that difficult whisper that escaped from his mouth, "I am your little muchacho."

He still had no expression, but I flushed, my chest tightened, and a smile spread over my face as I thought, You've got to be kidding.

Again, he struggled to say something, so I put my ear right up to his lips.

"I am back," he said.

The news spread faster than e-mail, and Amar Puri and Raghunath Puri were at Guru Ji's bedside in minutes. Hari Puri, however, had spoken enough for one day, and he just lay there like a baby, his eyes rolling in their sockets, still trying to focus. He didn't seem to know where he was. But he did.

While Kapil Puri Baba was in Jaipur, I had heard several conversations between him and Amar Puri, but their language was fast and furious, so I hadn't been able to grasp much. Bhairon Puri Baba's name kept coming up and often, in the same sentence and in close proximity, was the word *bahinchut* or what we may translate as *sister-fucker*. The other word I remembered was *tantric,* which Kapil Puri seemed to dismiss, waving his hands in the air.

12

A Question of Paths

Because we were now friends, I confronted Amar Puri Baba about his conversation with Kapil Puri Baba. He tried to change the subject, feigned ignorance, and even left the room for a while. But, eventually I got him to tell me that they had been talking about Datt Akhara. There had been a major rift in the Sixteen Lineages after Sandhya Puri Maharaj's death. Being his brilliant disciple and chosen successor to the throne of Datt Akhara, Hari Puri Baba should have been made the new *pir*, as the abbot of this sannyasi monastery was known. I found this title strange since *pir* is a Muslim term referring to a high Sufi teacher, not a Hindu one.

But the Council of Eight met, along with the trustees of Datt Akhara, and decided that Hari Puri was too young, while Gokarn Puri Baba had already spent fifty years living there. Besides, Gokarn Puri was ninety-one years old, and wouldn't live forever. They appointed Gokarn Puri Baba as abbot, but eighteen years had passed since then and he was still very much alive.

"Everyone living there at that time protested the decision, but when we saw that we were powerless to change it, we all left and have never returned. At the Kumbh in Ujjain, we camp outside Datt Akhara's gate!" Amar Puri explained.

Datt Akhara in Ujjain, is the ancient math of Juna Akhara. *Juna* means *old.* So before it was called the old akhara, when it was younger, it was called Datt Akhara, and even before that, Bhairon Akhara, after Shiva's terrifying form. Ujjain and Varanasi, are perhaps the two oldest still inhabited cities in the world. Ujjain goes back thousands of years, and the bards sing to us about Guru Dattatreya, himself, teaching his disciples on the very spot of Datt Akhara today, way back in the Treta Age, and worshipping the nearby Mahakal Bhairon Shivling with bhang and spirits. This Shiva linga is still considered one of the twelve *jyotilings,* phalluses of light. By the time Sandhya Puri Baba arrived at Datt Akhara, the once grand math had been reduced to the udambara tree surrounded by a few Shiva lingas and a dilapidated wooden bench.

Sandhya Puri was a nineteenth-century man. He was also a siddha, who remembered all his past lives, and Datt Akhara from previous ages, so when he first arrived in the present life, he couldn't believe that he was in the right place. There was a Muslim graveyard to one side, a swamp on the other, and the jungle, known for its tigers, on the third side. Datt Akhara was infested with snakes, scorpions, and malarial mosquitoes.

Sandhya Puri did manage to restore the math. He cleared the jungle, and drained the swamp, but when he asked the leaders of the Muslim community for the graveyard to be returned, their response was clear, "Our dead will lie there until the end of the world!"

The city fathers (who were among his devotees) tried to convince him to abandon a hopeless cause. Why stir up communal politics when none exist? There was no animosity between Hindus and Muslims in Ujjain in those days. But Sandhya Puri Baba took the case to the courts, to the guffaws of both Hindus and Muslims. This also did not go over well with the district collector, an Englishman, who first politely requested him to forget the whole thing and then cursed him when the baba respectfully refused to change his position.

Sandhya Puri had no deeds or legal claim on Datt Akhara, but only his personal memories from his past lives. However, he pointed out that while everyone assumed the property was a graveyard, there was no direct proof of that. The Muslims protested that countless fathers, mothers, brothers, and sisters were buried there, and there had been countless witnesses to these burials. "If that is the case," Sandhya Puri persisted, "then no one should object to us inspecting the alleged graves. Dig up one or two graves. If the bones are supine, as in a Muslim *kabr,* burial (in the same way as the dead are buried in the West), I will drop my claim in perpetuity. But if the corpses are sitting in a yoga posture (in the way sannyasis are buried), then the entire property should be turned over to Datt Akhara!" The Muslims, the judge, and the English collector sahib found this so ridiculous—to the point of being humorous—that they readily agreed, if only to put the matter to rest.

They were, therefore, shocked to see the corpses, from the first three graves and then (at the command of the incredulous collector), three more, all sitting upright, rosaries in hand, their dread locks intact. Yogi skeletons. *Shava-shakti.*

Several of the Muslim elders, without compromising their own religion, became staunch devotees of Sandhya Puri Baba, and were often seen in the akhara. Many other Muslims in Ujjain became his devotees, and addressed him by their Urdu Sufi term for the head of a Sufi order, *pir,* Father. From that time on, the Mahant of Datt Akhara has been called Pir.

It is said that there stood in the graveyard an old dargah, resembling a small mausoleum. No one knew who had been buried there. It had no inscription and was referred to simply as the dargah of the Old Pir. When Sandhya Puri had taken possession of the graveyard, he found a way to open it, and inside there was no corpse, lying or sitting, but a small black rock-throne on which lay two objects, barely recognizable as a pair of very small wooden sandals with a knob raised to fit between the large toe and the second one. Magic slippers, *padukas*.

Almost overnight, a majestic math arose where snakes had flourished—rooms, halls, a temple, an office, and sheds for a thousand cows. Datt Akhara was soon awash in an ocean of milk.

Not only were comfortable accommodations ready for them when the thousands of sadhus descended on Datt Akhara, but each sadhu was given new dhotis, sandals, blankets, a new brass kamandal made in Bhuj, a hundred-and-one-rupees dakshina, and several large *golis* of the finest Kashmiri hashish. The wealth seemed to appear out of nowhere. Although he never once looked at the books, Sandhya Puri maintained a balance sheet that zeroed out each and every day. And when he would donate a hundred gallons of milk to the poor, the cows' output would double.

Sandhya Puri Baba continued to sit naked on his deerskin, smoking the odd chillam, holding court. Sadhus, householders, Hindus, Muslims, beggars, and kings all came to him with their causes and their dreams. Everyone left Datt Akhara with something. A few left with miracles.

There was an ongoing debate about the source of the wealth. Many believed that the Mother of Cattle, also known as the Gift-Giving Cow, was responsible. Only few knew that it was the ancient padukas.

There were those who thought that perhaps some of the money ought to remain in the treasury for "great works." So, when Sandhya Puri left his body, fearing that Hari Puri would continue the generous ways of his guru, the council chose as pir Gokarn Puri who was a well-known miser.

However, the padukas disappeared.

"Bhairon Puri opposed your Guru Ji, and there has been bad feeling between them ever since. Bhairon Puri wants the *gaddi*-throne of Datt Akhara for himself. He's a bad sadhu, a tantric," said Amar Puri.

Not that all tantrics are bad. Contrary to what is known as a tantric in the New Age West (someone associated with sexual energy and practice), in the traditional world of India, a tantric is considered more a practitioner of magick arts, and in some cases, the Black Arts. Not that the goal of most tantrics is not that state some call Liberation, some call Enlightenment. It's a question of paths. In Tantra there is the Left-Hand Path and the Right-Hand Path. Red Bhairon Puri Baba pursued the Left-Hand Path with great determination and skill. "He poisoned Hari Puri!" said Amar Puri.

13

Hari Puri's Miraculous Return

I continued to massage my guru's fingers and toes and repeat the mantra that conquers death. Day and night. Hari Puri's breathing had changed; now it was deep and somewhat irregular when he slept. Each time he awoke, he seemed more alert.

"Your *mahamrtyunjaya* mantra won't be complete until you make a pilgrimage, a *yatra,*" said Hari Puri, one week after his return to full consciousness. "Perhaps an Amarnath Yatra." He was referring to the auspicious pilgrimage to the cave, Amarnath Gufa, fourteen thousand feet high in the Kashmir Himalayas, where Shiva imparted the knowledge of immortality to his consort, Parvati. Hari Puri's voice still wavered, and his eyes wobbled a little. "You think I don't know you were attempting this mantra while I was flying about? And he shouldn't have given you this mantra yet. First you must know other things, have other mantras—two others which I will give you."

Hari Puri couldn't move his body, and his face remained expressionless. He became a talking head. As he became stronger, as his eyes and voice steadied, his intense teachings began. He taught me about the greatest yogis, and singled out Shiva, Dattatreya, Ravan, Patanjali, and Panini. I found it very curious, even disturbing, that he emphasized that they were also the master grammarians of India.

"There are exactly seventy-two lakhs seventy-two thousand three hundred and eleven (7,272,311) *nadis* (subtle currents) in the human body. A yogi is someone who can count them all," Hari Puri explained.

Starting in the mid-1960s, I had devoured everything in English I could get my hands on about nadis, chakras, Kundalini, and auras. The books of C. W. Leadbetter of the somnambulant Theosophical Society stand out in my mind. I knew that nadis carried the five pranas, the vital energies (combustion-respiration-digestion, elimination, distribution-circulation, reaction-force, and planning-specialization), through the body. Yogis know how to control these energy flows so that the plexuses of the nadis, called *chakras,* which are like wheels and their spokes and are described as lotuses, open and this enables the vital force of nature, in the form of the snake goddess Kundalini, to rise upward to merge with pure consciousness, remove all ignorance, and realize the immortality of the soul.

But this was not what Hari Puri was talking about. How do you count nadis?

"First, you must be able to recognize a nadi and know exactly where it is. Then you must be able to distinguish one from another, so you don't count it twice," he continued. "A treasure map is not a treasure, even if the map *is* an authentic one." He squinted and frowned. "Most are forgeries, anyway. Those maps direct one to marks on the earth indicating some buried thing, marks that point at treasure. But maps approximate and paint a picture of a broken chain of marks, each one's proximity to another also an approximation that leads us from imaginary place to imaginary place, through space, in a particular sequence."

"The world, however, is the container of *all* things, and although all things are not known, they *are* marked. And they form an unbroken chain. I will show you a way to free yourself from the law of place, and without moving, transcend distance!

"Even with my eyes closed, even when I'm flying about, when I hear your voice in this hall of the dying, I know you are there, and I even know where you are. Your voice—that sound—marks your presence. Sounds can be marks of things both visible and invisible. Is distant thunder not the mark of an approaching storm? Is a fart not a mark of someone's poor digestion and an indication of the foul odor to come? Is a child's laughter not a mark of his bliss?

"Each nadi vibrates at a different speed, and as sound is perceived from vibration, each nadi has its own sound. Counting is not an exercise in ordering. When you count your mantras, using the hundred and eight beads on your rosary of rudrakshas, each is related to the next, and all of them are tied together by a *sutra,* a string, in sequence. In a similar way each sound has a relationship with all other sounds, and the sound of each of the 7,272,311 nadis has a relationship to each and all of the others. The law is a grammar that describes, but does not prescribe, how sounds combine to form the world. Our mundane world is comprised of many languages, but there is also a great language, and I'm not speaking of what they call Sanskrit, but a great grammar that reflects the creation, maintenance, and destruction of the universe. He who knows *that* grammar is a yogi."

Then he sang to me in his weakening voice:

> *jnanamrtam samarasam*
> *gaganopamoham*

"This is what I have to teach you. There is little time, so I am giving this to you, now. They are the words of Guru Dattatreya, and now my words. Later your words.

I am the vault of the heavens,
that, in perfect equanimity,
is amrit, the knowledge of immortality.

"There are marks embedded in the sounds you make that are reflected from that 'vault of the heavens.' The Yogi knows no difference between his voice and the vault of the heavens and so is able to create, maintain, and destroy the universe. Mind you, destruction of the universe is not a violent act accompanied by fire and explosions, but simply the disappearance of the web of illusion.

"In hatha yoga, the body assumes postures, asanas. No? In a similar way, we make asanas in our mouth, using breath and tongue. The resulting sounds are mantras. *Yam-Niyam-Asan!*" he said loudly, and I silently translated this as "discipline, prescription, and sitting." "The fourth is, of course, your Pranayam, with which you make sound with the breath.

"It's not what you do but what you say," Hari Puri whispered. "What escapes from the mouth can't be changed or taken back. Your tool of knowledge is language, because its boundaries establish the possibilities of the world."

"How do I practice this?" I asked, and I had all kinds of other questions, but he had already drifted off to sleep. I felt as if he had just entrusted me with a priceless jewel, so I walked across the street to the dharamsala to preserve this knowledge in the pages of my notebook.

The following day, I made applesauce by squeezing peeled and sliced apples through cloth but Hari Puri said that the glucose drip was sufficient. I insisted, and finally got him to take a little. I fed him with a spoon and, as I did so, I thought of the moment during my initiation when we fed each other raw sugar. Now, he was feeding my mind, and I was feeding his body. Amar Puri's ayurvedic remedies took considerably more coaxing before Hari Puri would swallow them. He wanted to know every ingredient, and then he would find some fault with it. "Do you think I'm trying to poison you?" Amar Puri would ask him.

The news of Hari Puri's miraculous return to the world spread quickly and devotees, sadhus, yogis, politicians, and even royalty arrived. There were more flowers in Dr. Rathor's TB ward than in Bombay's Crawford Market. The peeling pale green walls became a background for the orange and reds of marigolds and roses. "Give the roses to those who are sick," said Hari Puri. "I want only yellow!"

A cot was placed at Hari Puri's feet for Amar Puri and visiting sadhu dignitaries. Minstrels surrounded Hari Puri's bed, ringing their bells and singing his praises, those of Amar Puri, and babas of yore (often, I might add, to the tune of popular Hindi film songs). Devotees covered the floor like wall-to-wall carpeting, and the thick sweet smoke of chillams filled the ward and spilled out into the corridors and stairwells.

"You must think of me as a bodiless demon!" said Hari Puri one morning to Dr. Rathor who, during his rounds, would try to pretend our little scene didn't exist. Dr. Rathor's tense jaw loosened, as his frown rose into a brief smile. Rathor was a bright, well-meaning young man. He dreamed of making SMS Hospital a model of modern medicine but, as each day passed, his dream was becoming more remote. "This is a hospital!" he said finally as he finished writing a note on Hari Puri's chart. "Not a, uh . . . a temple!" He knew that he was losing control of the situation.

The crowds didn't give us much time alone, but we managed

to find two hours before the sun rose each day. My brain probably couldn't have handled any more than that. My guru was trying to teach me the unknowable and much of it was way over my head.

We retreated into a cave, under an ochre dhoti, and he taught me the basic *asanas*. He blew into my ears the mantra he claimed contained the whole universe:

> *om kakhagaghaṅa*
> *chachhajajhaña*
> *ṭaṭhaḍaḍhaṇa*
> *tathadadhana*
> *paphababhama*
> *yaralavasaṣasaha!*

"But I already know that, Guru Ji!" I protested.

"Do you now?" he questioned.

Was this one of Hari Puri's many jokes? I could never tell. "It's the Hindi alphabet . . ." I said, but before I could continue, he stopped me in my tracks.

"Alpha, Beta, Gamma and Ay, Bee, See are different. They are only the names of signs called 'letters' which are written down. They approximate the sounds they represent, but we are making asanas. Each syllable exactly marks the location of the posture. We move in an arc from the sound "uhhh" deep within the chest to "oo" which exits from the lips, or from the sound "ka" in the throat to "ma" produced by pursing the lips. This arc mirrors the vault of heaven. It is sacred geography."

This made me realize that sound is indeed linked to place, and that the practice of mantra is not so much a repetition of formulas, but yoga of the mouth.

When Hari Puri was ready to give me the next initiation into the Maheshwara Sutra, a pandit came and did a puja, a sacred ritual, just before sunrise. He tied a red string around my wrist, and Guru Ji's as well.

Shiva Nataraj, in his manifestation as Lord of the Dance, dances to the rhythm of his own drum. Dancing is unlike walking or running in that you don't go anywhere. At the end you are where you were at in the beginning. Shiva doesn't go anywhere and he doesn't create anything. He doesn't maintain anything and he doesn't destroy anything. The destruction of the universe is merely the collapse of illusion. Shiva's dance is pure movement, a play of consciousness, but from the rhythm of the drum comes the seeds of language beginning with his five-syllable mantra:

om nama shivaya!

And from that manifests Shiva's Maheshwara Sutra Mantra. All human knowledge stems from the Maheshvara Sutra Mantra. So I was told, and then given the sacred syllables.

From the infant's first sound, an experimental and unformed *a*, pronounced like the vowel in "hut," springs all the sounds of his life. I became an infant once more, but this time, instead of mimicking my mother, my gurgles and new sounds were my attempts to come to terms with this new world where sound is place. He took me through the vault of heaven (or was it my vocal arc?), stopping at each station along the way, to learn the name of each by listening to the sound coming from my own mouth.

I had brought my notebook, but he objected. "I want to be able to study and memorize the system," I explained.

"This isn't something to study," he said, "or even something to have faith in. You go to the right place in your body, control your breath and your touch, and you are there. It unfolds itself. It's not a system."

I had to drop the idea of letters and the different sounds they represented. In the Extraordinary World there are just the sounds of syllables, which double as their names. I was told that there was no room for error, that I mustn't mispronounce a single syllable.

On some days Hari Puri's mood would turn sour, like some of the apples that devotees brought me. "What? You think the Rishi Patanjali and the Rishi Panini were sitting in some Angrezi university, teaching in great halls, writing books published at university expense? You think that they had ideas that just came into their heads, that they did research?" he said one day. "You will never understand these things.

"No, these men were great sadhus who lived at their dhunis surrounded by disciples who didn't spend their time studying, but selflessly serving their gurus. And the gurus gave to their disciples what they had received from their own gurus. Not just the 'teachings,' or instruction, but the gurus transferred their own nature, so that the very personality of the guru became that of the disciple. With this as a foundation, these seeds of knowledge you call 'teachings,' when passed down bore fruit, and that fruit bears more seeds. This is the tradition."

Shortly after Hari Puri's return to consciousness, Kapil Puri Baba left Jaipur. He took the train down to Ujjain, to visit Datt Akhara for the first time in eighteen years, since Gokarn Puri Baba had been made Pir. He was shocked by what he saw. Sadhu Heaven was no more. Datt Akhara had crumbled and deteriorated into a memory.

"The padukas disappeared," was Gokarn Puri's excuse to Kapil Puri, who could see no trace of the former prosperity. He shouted,

Praises to Shiva!
Giver of food, drink, and smoke.

Clearing the brambles and stones
You oppress the misers.

Kapil Puri then lit a chillam and exhaled a dark cloud of smoke.

"As the smoke from my chillam dissipates, so shall any memory of your overlordship of Datt Akhara fade! May you find the padukas in a future life! Insh'Allah!" he heckled the old man.

It so happened that Bhairon Puri Baba was also staying for a few days at the math. He agreed with Kapil Puri on Gokarn Puri's incompetence. "He will die, soon," Bhairon Puri said. "I can read it. I could probably tell you the day . . ."

Kapil Puri asked whether he planned to use his tantric powers to kill him off.

"Hey, he's a hundred years old! There's no need for that! Who do you think I am, anyway? All I want is your blessing. With that, I shall restore Datt Akhara to its former glory," Bhairon Puri responded.

"What about the padukas?" questioned Kapil Puri.

"You know where they are. Hari Puri has them," said Bhairon Puri.

Eventually, things at SMS hospital really got out of hand. Ash-covered naked yogis now slept on the floor at night and for their afternoon siesta. Amar Puri sat on his cot at Hari Puri's feet and distributed prasad and ayurvedic medicines, which he made across the street, to one and all. Even the other TB patients, seeing Hari Puri's miraculous return to life, replaced their antibiotics with Amar Puri's magic herbs. And they seemed to get better! Dr. Rathor found this even more disturbing than the fact that his beloved TB ward had become an ashram. He was humiliated, and I felt bad for him. His nicely ordered world was crumbling before his very eyes. I talked to Hari Puri about this, and he told me there were things I just couldn't understand but that everything would work out for the best. Nevertheless, he explained that we had outstayed our welcome, and it was time to go.

Arjun Singh was a gentle beast of a man, a lay devotee with a lion's mane of thick black hair. He brought the jeep from Amloda Kund, carefully lifted Hari Puri out of his bed, and carried him down the stairs as if he were a baby. He would do anything for Baba. He had been a dacoit, a highwayman, until one day Guru Ji convinced him that he wasn't smart enough to be a gangster or a politician, which is any dacoit's ultimate goal.

We decided to take Hari Puri Baba to an ashram in Jaipur rather than return to Amloda Kund. "I want to die in my own ashram!" Hari Puri said, but he was overruled. Our invitation promised royal treatment, and we accepted.

I had become tired of sleeping under Guru Ji's bed on the hard hospital floor, and now enjoyed a cot with a cotton mattress and the tranquil and pastel-colored dreams it produced. The noise of the traffic and the hacking and spitting of the ward was a thing of the past and Guru Ji now had a large wooden platform beside my cot. When I had a little time off, I explored the ashram's gardens and shrines and the mini observatory.

Hari Puri's strength rapidly increased, his voice became strong and authoritative, and he could even shake his head "no" when someone came with his herbal medicine. One day I found him wiggling his fingers. And with pillows and bolsters, he was able to sit up, but still his legs didn't work.

"I'd like to be able to take you with me where I go . . ." he said, "when you and the rest of the world are asleep. If I were a proper sadhu, I would have died at the Kumbh. It was the right moment, but Madhu Giri agreed to take my place. Before discarding this body, I wanted to have some fun, so I left my body in your very capable hands and became a tourist. I flew to all the tirths, all the sacred places—to Kashmir, Kerala, Bengal, Dwarka Ji—everywhere I had visited before and more. I had never seen Golden Lanka, for example," he said. "I sacrificed my legs to grow wings!

"The other patients in the hospital also flew around at night but rarely left the ward. They bounced off the walls, looking for the way out, but they couldn't find it, and so they died. Because I have sinned, now I too must relinquish this body," he said. "I have no use for it anymore."

It upset me to hear him talk like this. "You've never sinned in your entire life, Baba Ji!" I argued, associating this word *sin* with Christianity and redemption.

"What do you know, child?" he asked. "What do you know of sin? You are much too young. It's the sounds one makes during his life. The actions that follow are only remnants of those sounds, pieces that fall off, like chopped-off hands, but once those sounds are articulated, once they leave the lips, they never return but become an inseparable part of a harmony or a dissonance that is the world. Sin is mispronunciation."

"But you will get stronger, and get the use of your legs back. Together we'll visit all the pilgrimage places on foot. We'll explore the universe, make secret formulations of rare herbs, chart the heavens, and build ashrams! There is so much you still have to teach me, and I'll be the perfect disciple," I said.

"No, that won't be possible. Time's up. The whistle has blown.

"I want you to leave me tomorrow morning," he said. "Shhh-sh! I am going to die, and I don't want you to be here when it happens, so you must go. It is important that you remember me as I am now."

The room spun, and I felt nauseous. He couldn't be serious, but he was. It was final.

I shook my head again and again. "What do you mean?" I asked him, but he didn't answer. "If you're going to die, Guru Ji, I'll stay and take care of you."

"You've completed your seva, your selfless service, now go, move on. You have more important things to do now," he said without any emotion.

"But I don't want to leave you!" I protested.

"This is the last *ajna,* command, that I'll give you. I think you should obey it. And besides, don't worry, I will never leave you," he said, and attempted a smile.

Holding back my despair, I performed my omkars in front of Hari Puri Baba, and then buried my face in his feet.

I would never see him again—in his body.

14

Gangotri Baba

Even though I was never able to come to grips with the fact that Hari Puri Baba sent me away when he was dying, I could understand him wanting me to remember him in a certain way. At least that's how I felt when I left Rajasthan. He ordered me to leave so abruptly that I thought his death was imminent. I feared that my discipleship had ended, and felt an emptiness possess me. I hadn't learned enough or found the deep secrets I was after. I had blown my big chance.

I crisscrossed India visiting temples and babas during a year of wanderlust that finally deposited me at the dhuni of Ganga Giri Baba, known as Gangotri Baba, in the Kumaun Himalayas, near the eastern border of Nepal. Tall, emaciated, crowned with dreadlocks, and covered in ashes, he could have frightened off any ghost from any cremation ground. He was a tantric and a healer. And he was quite mad, but I felt perfectly at home.

When I first arrived, I spent a few nights sleeping at the dhuni, but when it appeared I intended to stay a while, Gangotri Baba showed me a nearby cave, which became my home for the next couple of months.

I would spend my mornings and evenings with Gangotri Baba,

but we were rarely alone. People came from far and wide, some to be healed but most of them for help with invisible powers. Some wanted success, riches, sons, victory in an undertaking, or revenge. Others suspected malevolent interference in their lives from human, ghost, or god.

Often, a man would approach the dhuni, and Gangotri Baba, brandishing his long iron tongs, would threaten him with dire consequences should he move a step closer. Surprised at Baba's aggressive behavior, I would ask him who the man was. "A ghost," he would say. Like Hari Puri Baba, he was literate and could read the signs.

I was surprised to hear the locals referring to Gangotri Baba as Patrick Baba. He had been born into a good Indian Christian family, and received an English name. He was sent to the best schools, and then to medical school, and became an allopathic (Western) doctor. He was also a passionate boxer, and having a large build, was able to knock out all his opponents. Perhaps it wasn't the boxing, but the intensity behind it that changed his world. He killed a man in the ring.

Neither charged nor convicted of a crime, he left his home in Nainital and the medical profession, and wandered for months (or was it years) before he found himself at the cremation ghat on the Jamuna River in Delhi. There he met a woman, a yogini, who possessed great powers. As he put it, "She took me 'airmail' to Assam, first to get the blessings of the Mother Goddess, Kamakhya Devi, and then to the jungle."

Gangotri Baba's new family became the Naga gurus and gurubhais in Juna Akhara. He went on long fasts as his unkempt hair turned to rope and fell to the ground. He discarded all semblance of clothing and began an intense study of Ayurveda, homeopathy, and tantric practices. With the same ferocity he had used to kill a man, he now protected all God's creatures.

Often, he would complete his medical diagnosis quickly by look-ing at a patient's eyes or tongue, or checking their pulse. He might write a prescription or retrieve herbs or medicinal ashes from his many tins and jars. But, sometimes, he would suspect foul play, and send his pals, the crows, on reconnaissance missions to the homes of the affected and possessed.

The crows loved Gangotri Baba as much as they did Hari Puri. Both babas conversed with the crows and fed them prasad. "Crows chase away all the other birds, so sometimes I have to tell them to go away for a while," he would say. But when he called them with his shrill scream, they would appear instantly, standing at attention at the dhuni, ready for duty.

One morning, a particularly distraught-looking man walked into our clearing, touched Baba's feet, and sat down at a distance. His clothes were neglected and unwashed, his hair disheveled, and the stubbly beard growing on his face looked like weeds in a discarded field. "Go down to the river and wash your clothes, man!" Gangotri Baba scolded. The man followed his instructions and reappeared an hour later, fresh and clean, but still looking dispirited.

He explained to Baba that since his father had died, one calam-ity after another had fallen on his family. His crops failed several years in a row, their water source had dried up, and now each of his sons had fallen ill. Baba told him to return to his home and wait for the crows to come. "How will they know where to go?" the farmer asked. "They see from above. They watch the action." Gangotri Baba said, "When they arrive at your home, watch what they do, where they go. If they peck the ground, then dig in that very spot. If you find anything, bring it to me."

Several days later, the farmer returned with a red cloth bundle. "These things were buried in four places around the house," the man explained. I moved close to Baba to see what the man had found.

There was twisted human hair, human nails, torn swatches of cloth eaten by white ants, twigs including several from the neem tree that were used to brush teeth, and a couple of five-paisa coins.

"The Earth is full of hidden things," said Baba before intoning mantras and sprinkling drops of water over the accursed items. "Fire reveals things with its light, and causes darkness to vanish," Baba said. He awakened the coals in the dhuni until it smoked and flamed. He made a circle of turmeric powder around it and decorated his trident and tongs with green chile peppers and more turmeric root, all the while intoning his mantras. Then he enraged the flames with myrrh and ghee. I was forced to back away from the intense heat. "To the cremation pyre!" he yelled, and tossed the items the man had brought into the inferno. Now he stood up and appeared like Mahakal Bhairav, the wrathful manifestation of the Great God Shiva; there was madness in his face.

Slowly, he circled the sacred fire with a lemon hidden in his large, bony hand, and, like a great cat stalking its prey, he approached his trident in the northeast corner of his dhuni. He was in trance. Everyone backed away in fear. This baba could do *anything*. He no longer saw his human audience, but looked all around with large paranoid eyes, as if he were about to hide a treasure in a secret place. When he appeared to be satisfied that he was completely alone, he impaled the lemon on the center spoke of the trident with urgent finality. No one breathed. Gangotri Baba returned to his place behind the dhuni, pulled some hashish from under his tiger skin, and threw it at the farmer with a Cavendars cigarette. "Make me a chillam," he said, "and all your problems will be over!"

"When you spiked the lemon did you kill the black magician?" I asked him the following day. "Of course not!" he replied. "I simply reflected the perpetrator's little tantra back onto him. A reflection of an illusion!" he laughed. "But illusions can be very dangerous."

He asked no payment for his services but demanded loyalty for continued services. "Come for darshan every once in a while," he would say. "Send me a letter, a card. No need of extravagant gifts, just make sure there is 'something' for the dhuni."

I asked Baba if he could give me something for my flatulence. Perhaps it was the unfiltered river water I was drinking. He showed me the boils on his legs. "I can't cure my own boils," he told me. "If you cure my boils, I'll cure your gas. Every time I heal someone, I get boils. The stronger the disease, the longer the boils last. I don't know why I put myself through this. All for these ungrateful idiots who go out and get sick again."

"What they call Ayurveda is not Ayurveda," Gangotri Baba said to me one day, while speaking to a learned pandit. "This wise Brahmin tells me he has exhausted the treasure house of Ayurveda, in searching for a cure for his beloved wife. He has gone to all the great healers without any result, and I am his last hope." Baba laughed and then turned to the pandit to lecture him. "You don't know the first thing about Ayurveda, Pandit Ji," he said, "Now, go home, and standing on the north side of your house, walk north until you come to the first mango tree. It doesn't matter whether it is ten meters or ten kilometers. Climb up the tree and pick three of the topmost leaves. Then return home, and sitting on your threshold, place the three leaves in a chillam, and smoke them. Your wife will be cured."

And the wife was cured, but the disease, probably cancer, was so powerful that not only did Baba get large and cancerous-looking boils on his legs, but I got them as well. The pandit was ecstatic, and brought flowers, fruits, and sweets from the finest sweet shop in Nainital, and a gift of money. Baba accepted the gifts but told the pandit in the most abusive language to leave us alone to suffer our boils in private. Afterward, Baba told me that the gifts would only make the boils worse.

Baba would often bring up the subject of the merchant who came to him with a case of the evil eye. Impressed with the success of Baba's exorcism, the merchant brought gifts and asked for blessings that would result in the success of his business. And successful he was, outgrowing his small town, moving to Nainital, and striking it rich. He gradually forgot about Gangotri Baba. "Then, I had to turn the screw a little to the left," Baba would say, and I cringed when I heard those words.

My decision to leave Gangotri Baba had little to do with those words, even if they did echo in my head. What does he mean by that, anyway? He told me that if I wanted him to give me hidden teachings, I should take guru mantra from him. But I already had my guru mantra that was the focus of my practice, and through it my lineage and family. Gangotri Baba was an eccentric uncle, an astounding yogi, but not my guru. Besides, what would happen to me if I were a bad chela?

After I left Gangotri Baba, I was lucky enough to find a small abandoned temple, not far from the old Eppworth Estate, just north of Almora, that an old friend, Donny M., had rented, and was awaiting Timothy Leary, the infamous professor from Harvard University who was encouraging America's middle class youth to "tune in, turn on, and drop out."

Leary had recently escaped from a federal prison in California with the aid of the Black Panthers, fled the United States, and was slowly making his way to India. Someone had contacted Donny, and asked him to rent Eppworth, where, I believe, Leary had camped out several years earlier and wrote *The Psychedelic Experience*, based on the Tibetan Book of the Dead. Leary had fond memories of Almora, and wanted to return for some peace and a chance to reflect on things.

It was the maharaja of Kashmir, the spiritual Dr. Karan Singh, who originally invited Leary to India, offering the hospitality that went with Dr. Singh's stature. He had been interested for many years in mind-altering substances, and corresponded with Aldous Huxley on the effects of mescaline. Turning down an invitation to visit India because of his poor health (he passed away shortly thereafter), Huxley suggested that he contact this young professor at Harvard, Dr. Leary, who could, perhaps, supply him with mescaline or something else. The rest is history, or rather mythology.

Because my little temple had no door, I hung a straw mat over the entrance when I slept and during my infrequent forays into the world beyond the jungle, mainly to Eppworth. I had no valuables to speak of but, considering my finances, losing my cooking pots would have been devastating. Besides, I had my notebook (which had grown to three volumes) and the nectar water pot Hari Puri had given me. My bag-of-wishes was always on my shoulder when I went out. Guarding against possible thieves added to my resolve to sit and meditate until something significant happened.

Almora has a history of foreigners coming for spiritual retreat and then settling on the beautiful mountainside. There was the Englishman, Krishna Prem, the German, Lama Anagarika Govinda, the Dane, Sunyata, the Englishman, Buddhananda, the Frenchman, Alain Daniélou, and many others. Mary Obligger, an American Quaker from Pennsylvania, had come in 1956 with her husband, a Swiss ecologist working for the United Nations. Mary became everyone's mother, baking cookies and apple pie for anyone who just might happen to stop by. I was one of her regular visitors.

She told me the secret of her own vigor and longevity was drinking her urine. I was ready to try anything just to be able to sit comfortably on the hard ground. I followed her precise instructions and within a week, not only had my boils disappeared, but also I felt a renewed strength. I kept up the unsocial practice for forty days, which made me even more of a recluse.

The day I completed my cure, the boy who delivered milk in the morning told me that a doctor with strange medicines, (pointing to his head), had arrived at Eppworth. I took this to be Dr. Leary and went to investigate. However, it turned out to be not the psychedelic guru but his Almora equivalent, Dr. Bindu. Inspired by his hallucinatory experiences during Leary's earlier visit, Dr. Bindu had begun researching the mind-altering botanicals of India. He had searched ancient texts, collected a wide variety of plants, and could be found in his laboratory until the wee hours. His instant nirvana pill failed to produce any spectacular results but enabled us to stay awake all night talking. At dawn, I returned to my temple.

When I saw that my straw mat was missing from the entrance, I got a sinking feeling in my stomach and began to curse myself for staying out all night. As I got closer, I heard some commotion inside. The thieves are still there, I thought, and, picking up a rock, I burst inside.

"*Om Namo Narayan!*" said Kedar Puri Baba, as he rose from my thin stuffed cotton mattress. "Wow!" I exclaimed, as we each made a gesture to touch each other's feet that turned into a warm embrace.

"How did you find me here?" I asked incredulously. "Guru Ji . . ." he started to say, but I stopped him. "I know why you're here," I said, "it's written all over your face."

"We have no time, Rampuri," he said. "It wasn't easy to find you. The feast is in a couple of days. It will take that long to get there." By the "feast" he meant the traditional bhandara on the fourteenth day after the death that served as a wake as well as occasion of the distribution of property. "I have no money," I told him. "Amar Puri Baba gave me money to bring you," Kedar Puri Baba said, "and maybe there will be some left over." I agreed that we should leave within the hour. "I hope there's enough money for me to get back here," I said. "I'll just come for a few days."

That was the first reason why I didn't meet Timothy Leary in Almora. The second was that before he could leave Kabul on the bus that would take him through the Khyber Pass to Peshawar, Pakistan, American FBI agents swooped in on him in his hotel, arrested him, and returned him to America to complete his prison sentence.

"Is it true, Ram Puri bhai," asked Kedar Puri as we descended the mountains, "that the streets in Am-rika are paved with gold? Does everyone live in great palaces? Do they all eat from golden plates and drink from silver goblets encrusted with priceless gems? Let's go there after the feast for Guru Ji."

15

The Ghost of Hari Puri Baba

"I can keep you alive forever," Amar Puri Baba had told Hari Puri Baba in Jaipur, suggesting that they should move to the Hanuman temple in Siloda, Madhya Pradesh. But Hari Puri Baba wanted to leave his body in Amloda Kund.

"I don't want, I don't need this body, anymore," Hari Puri replied.

"But we need you," said Amar Puri. "Without you, how can the padukas be restored to the sacred throne of Datt Akhara? Is Siloda not close to Ujjain? I will heal you in Siloda, and from there we will all return to Datt Akhara."

"Why should I be healed? This body is finished," Hari Puri Baba said. "I'll take another one, if you need me so much, but why don't you just let me go?"

Everyone present touched their earlobes, and joined their hands together in front of their faces.

"Please don't talk like that, Guru Ji," said one of the devotees.

"Okay, I'll go to Siloda to die, and you can install a statue of me, there." Hari Puri was known for his ability to solve disputes by compromise. "But I must see it completed."

"It's just not done that way," Amar Puri Baba pleaded when Hari Puri insisted that his statue be carved from marble while he was still alive.

However, Hari Puri drove a hard bargain.

Amar Puri took him to Siloda in the jeep driven by Arjun Singh. It was very dusty, the roads were bad, and the jeep had no suspension.

Kedar Puri explained all this to me during our two-and-a-half-days' journey to Siloda on a long series of buses. The day the statue was finished in Jaipur, Hari Puri Baba left his body in Siloda. Word was sent out all over North India with the news of his passing, mainly by "jungle telegraph" or "soul wire." According to Indian tradition, fourteen days after the death a wake is held, his life celebrated, and his property distributed.

The last twenty miles were excruciating, first in a broken-down bus on a non-road and then in a bullock cart that took us the rest of the way. By the time we arrived, it must have been around 9 p.m., and darkness covered the ashram like a thick wool blanket. A devotee greeted us with a kerosene lantern that provided faint illumination only on the ground in front of us. Kedar Puri took me by the hand and led me to the dhuni where Amar Puri Baba was sitting in meditation.

Out of the darkness, voices greeted us,

om namo narayan!

I became filled with emotion, and my eyes brimmed with tears. Somehow I had never believed that Hari Puri would leave his body.

Amar Puri Baba forced a smile as I performed my omkars and placed dakshina under his foot. I put my forehead on his feet, and I felt his little tap, an espresso hit of shaktipat, where my neck joined my head. And then Kedar Puri walked me over to the tomb and left me there.

Because I couldn't see anything, I used my sense of touch to locate myself in front of the earth rising in a mound. I performed my omkars and then rested my hands on the grave as if it were Hari Puri's feet. I repeated my guru mantra and imagined his blessings coming up from the earth below. Hari Puri Baba had been entombed in salt, sitting in samadhi with a rosary of rudraksha seeds in his right hand.

Crickets and other insects buzzed about in the oppressive atmosphere. I had the sense that an unseasonal storm was brewing. "What now, Guru Ji?" I asked out loud.

But it wasn't the sudden explosion of thunder, nor the crack and flash of the lightning that followed, that startled me. I jumped back when the lightning revealed the ghost of a scowling Hari Puri Baba sitting on a throne. A sharp pain shot through my body as my coccyx connected with the sharp corner of the unfinished brick wall surrounding the tomb. My knees buckled and I fell back with a grunt.

One of Amar Puri's devotees approached, holding a lantern above his head and hung it from a branch. The ghost of Hari Puri Baba was still visible, but now I realized that it was a white marble statue of him.

I told myself to calm down. The wind caused the lantern to flicker, and as it did so, Hari Puri appeared to blink his eyes several times, turn his head, and change his expression. I saw anger, happiness, sarcasm, love, and heavenly bliss as one expression morphed into the next.

"I'm trapped in this statue, child," he said to me inside my head. "Do you think this damn thing looks anything like me?" he asked. "Free me," he commanded, but I was clearly talking to myself.

I studied the statue. Now its expression was frozen and did not look happy to me. "Should I have another statue made for your tomb?" I asked him.

"Yes, that would be good for starters," he said.

Kedar Puri Baba caught me and shook me out of my reverie as I made my way back to Amar Puri Baba. Because there were many sadhus still arriving, he pulled me over to a huge canopy and suggested that we claim some sleeping space while it was still available. I hadn't expected such a large event.

"You must stay here, at our guru's samadhi, for at least two years, until next Kumbh Mela in Hardwar," Kedar Puri said.

"I'll do whatever I want," I replied, suddenly irritated.

"It's your duty, Rampuri," he said.

"You talk rubbish!" I heard myself saying to him in a raised angry voice. "Who do you think you are? My guru? He's dead."

Kedar Puri stepped back, as bewildered by my outburst as I was. What had come over me? I wanted to apologize, but self-righteousness wouldn't allow it. What gave him the right to interfere with my headspace? I was right there, talking to my deceased Guru Ji, and suddenly Kedar Puri's interference.

"Rampuri, I was just trying to show you the right way . . ." That did it.

"Why do you destroy my peace of mind, my bliss? Useless fellow! Only trouble-making, I tell you!" I barked, my choice of words odd, and my tongue out of control. He walked away, and my mood soured. I felt like Hari Puri Baba's statue looked, frozen and grumpy.

The following day saw the great luminaries of Juna Akhara arrive from all over North India, but Amar Puri refused to leave the dhuni and wouldn't speak to anyone. He ignored me as well until I gave him the large ball of hashish I had brought from Almora. This brought a momentary smile to his face. He cut it, smelled it, and threw a piece to Kedar Puri Baba to make a chillam.

"Now that he is gone, there is no authority left. They are all jockeying for power. What power? There is only dharma," Amar Puri Baba said. "If I could have, I would have bowed to that man. Sandhya Puri Baba made him a sannyasi, but I made him a Naked One. I performed that final initiation. From now on I will bow to no human authority."

He tried to produce another smile and failed. "So, what are you going to do now that your guru is gone?" he asked.

"But aren't you also my guru?" I asked him, but the way he turned away from me was not a good sign. I got the feeling that he didn't take me seriously.

Like a cat suddenly perceiving movement, Amar Puri Baba's head turned, and he watched Red Bhairon Puri approach and then walk away, muttering under his breath when he saw that Amar Puri would not even acknowledge his presence.

After he had departed, sounds erupted from Amar Puri's mouth like the earth belching up poisonous gas. "Why is he here?" he said. "Did he want to make sure that Hari Puri Baba was indeed dead and buried?"

After the chillam had made its rounds, everyone left, and Kedar Puri signaled me to leave Baba alone, but I ignored him. Amar Puri Baba turned to me and cleaned his whiskers. "And what business do you have here?" he asked.

I knew that Hari Puri Baba had quarreled with Red Bhairon Puri over my initiation and that Bhairon Puri had threatened him. Then, the moment I became a sannyasi, Hari Puri had been stricken and lapsed into a coma. I had never considered the implications of this before, and now I wondered if Amar Puri blamed me for Hari Puri's death. Was I indeed responsible?

"You and Hari Puri Baba are to me like two bodies connected

to one soul," I said to Amar Puri. "Let me stay here and serve you, as I did for Guru Ji," I heard myself say, automatically canceling my plans to return to Almora. Am I a complete idiot, I thought to myself; my duty is here with Amar Puri Baba. "I still have so much to learn," I said.

"What can I teach you?" he asked. "You speak hardly any Hindi, and you have a strange way of thinking. I don't think I could ever make you understand anything. If you were Indian, it would be different."

I could see his point. I was an outsider. But how does the outsider become an insider?

"The padukas must be returned to their rightful owner," claimed Red Bhairon Puri.

I couldn't understand most of what was being said, but I did understand that. I sat at the edge of a large circle of sadhus and heard myself mutter under my breath that the padukas belong to Lord Dattatreya. Kedar Puri Baba dug me in the ribs. Bhairon Puri stopped, cocked his head, and looked in my direction.

"What did the Angrez say?" he asked.

"He was just talking to himself in English," said Kedar Puri. "Probably some stupid thing."

"I want to know what he said," Bhairon Puri insisted.

Kedar Puri tried to get me to leave, but my feet were cemented to the ground.

"Tell me, Angrez!" Bhairon Puri shouted. Clasping my hands together in front of my face, I closed my eyes and tried to make myself disappear. I heard Kapil Puri tell Bhairon Puri that if he had a bone to pick, he was ready for him. Why make a fuss about a foreigner, who obviously knew nothing about nothing?

"Maybe the Angrez has some useful information?"

The heat in my face spread through my body until I was on fire. Why doesn't he just use his tantric powers to find the padukas, I wondered.

"Yes, he's a powerful tantric," Kapil Puri Baba, one of Hari Puri's closest guru-brothers, said later, "but so is Arjun Puri Baba, and so am I! After the Kumbh, when Bhairon Baba asked for a meeting with Baba Ji, the leader of all us Puris in the Juna Akhara, Baba Ji agreed on condition that they sit in the air two feet above the ground. I was the witness to their debate, but out of respect I sat lower than Baba Ji. He is my guru, you know. Bhairon Baba said that time was the ultimate illusion, and as soon as he said that, we all mocked him for stating the obvious. Bhairon Baba stormed out of the room, swearing to take revenge. He believes that Hari Puri Baba took the padukas and that you might know where he hid them," he said.

"I don't even know what they look like," I said, hoping he would tell me about them.

"The padukas are the sign of discipleship and knowledge and therefore Dattatreya, himself. They are his wooden sandals that connect him to the Earth, in the same way that knowledge connects with discipleship and spirit with matter. We touch our guru's feet because they too are connected to the Earth. It is a link in a chain, a place where two worlds meet, a crossing over. So whenever Dattatreya takes a body, and he does so from time to time, he leaves his padukas as his signature. These padukas were brought to Ujjain from Multan, in what is now Pakistan, by Keshav Puri Baba, whose other name is Multani Baba. And it is our family that has been entrusted with Datt Akhara and the ancient knowledge that haunts the graves of the great yogis buried there."

As Kapil Puri Baba continued with his stories of Multani Baba and others in the lineage, I became enchanted by this yogi, who, when he pulled his moustache Indian-hero style, seemed more like a renegade general. He possessed the Ocean of Story. So when he invited me to return with him to Kashi, I accepted immediately.

"You must learn Sanskrit," he said. "I'll have you tutored by the finest pandits in Kashi. You will live with me in the Akhara, and I'll make you into a real sadhu."

"What do the padukas look like, Baba Ji, just in case I run across them?"

"They are ancient, the wood looks like honeycomb, and they are small enough for a child," said Kapil Puri.

The following day, I followed the large crowd to the gate of the ashram, where a jeep had arrived from Ujjain with the hundred and twelve-year-old Gokarn Puri Baba. Pir Ji, as he was called, was lifted out of the jeep and, supported by two babas, walked slowly to an oversized chair in front of the mound that entombed Hari Puri.

Juna Akhara's president-secretary, Shri Mahant Arjun Puri, and Bhairon Puri took their places next to the throne, but the chair for Amar Puri Baba remained empty because he refused to leave the dhuni. Amar Puri's absence caused a moral dilemma because Gokarn Puri was his guru. How could an enlightened soul, immersed in Dharma, not honor his own guru? Raghunath Puri Baba and other senior brothers went to counsel him.

"I will not participate if Bhairon Puri is there," said Amar Puri Baba.

"Dishonor the man, if you must, but not the seat of power," said one of the babas. As I learned later, the art of practicing Dharma includes knowing how and when to compromise. After the signs have been interpreted, appropriate action is taken in light of the circumstances and context.

Amar Puri stretched like a cat, and with small slow strides, walked over to Gokarn Puri Baba. The sea of sitting babas parted. He placed eleven rupees in his ancient teacher's lap, put his hands together, said his omkars, and returned to the dhuni. He had paid his respects and his religious fees but had not touched the Pir's feet. Kapil Puri Baba sat down in Amar Puri's chair.

I tried to avoid the Pir's gaze. I felt like Jack, who had climbed the beanstalk and was hiding in the corner of the giant's palace. He might suspect that I wanted to steal the gold, but I didn't know where it had been hidden and had no intentions of stealing anything.

After the feast was served, Hari Puri's few bundles of rupee notes were distributed. Kapil Puri Baba took charge as Amar Puri stayed by the dhuni. I sat with Amar Puri as one great yogi after another praised the life and achievements of Hari Puri Baba. At one point, Amar Puri broke his silence. "You use the word, *yogi* again and again," he said to the crowd. "But what does that mean? Who is a 'yogi'?" He looked into their eyes. "He who has no self-interest is a yogi. Hari Puri Baba was such a man."

Kedar Puri sat down beside me. I was sorry that I had given him such a hard time. I knew that he loved me as a brother, and I remembered that I had promised Hari Puri the last time I had seen him alive that I would always look after Kedar Puri because he needed someone. "He is a first-class rascal," Hari Puri Baba had said.

"You're a first-class rascal! Where's the rest of the money?" I heard myself say as Kedar Puri Baba handed me a thousand rupees. I felt uncomfortable accusing my guru-bhai of being a thief without any evidence but, as it turned out, Kedar Puri had indeed been caught with his hand in the cookie jar. He took another five hundred odd rupees from his bag-of-wishes and offered it to me.

"Keep it," I said, "I have enough." He is a rascal, I thought, but a lovable one.

As soon as the bhandara ended, the sadhus put their bedrolls over their shoulders and hit the road. I summoned up my courage to tell Amar Puri that I would be going to Kashi with Kapil Puri, that he was going to give me some training and I would study Sanskrit.

"You do whatever you think best," he said, "but how can you begin a new enterprise on a Tuesday? How will you learn anything if the Hanuman inside you is afflicted by Mangal-Mars?" I didn't know exactly what he meant, but I knew that Tuesday, Mars-day, was an inauspicious day to start something.

"Besides," he said, examining the lines on my forehead and the shape of my nose, "have you no regard for Brhaspati-Jupiter, the Guru of the Gods, whose star, Punarvasu, is inscribed on your face? Don't you know how to read the signs? Besides, child," he said softly, "you remind me of Hari Puri Baba, and I miss him. Stay with me for a little while, and I will show you some things."

I went to the jeep where Kapil Puri Baba was waiting for me and explained that I needed to remain at the ashram. Kapil Puri laughed.

"This is the middle of nowhere, boy," he said. "I'm inviting you to come to Kashi, the center of the universe."

I explained that it my duty to stay with Amar Puri and that I would follow him to Kashi later. He opened the door of the jeep and took my head in his hands.

"Remember that the padukas were Multani Baba's," he whispered to me. "When Sandhya Puri Baba found them, Multani Baba entered his body. He forbade Sandhya Puri to give them to Gokarn Puri, so when Sandhya Puri left his body, Gokarn Puri got the sacred throne of Datt Akhara but not the padukas."

16

The Process of Un-Becoming

In becoming a baba, it is substance that creates form. In becoming a baba quickly, substance is impossible, so form has to suffice until substance finally shows its face. When I started my discipleship with Amar Puri, I was very rough indeed, despite having all the trappings of a baba.

I tried desperately to blend in, so I was always aware of how I sat, the position of my hands and feet, how I received prasad or a chillam, how I drank water and tea, the way I arrived, and the way I departed. My attention was often on how I was being perceived by the community. But my movements, my voice, and my logic continually betrayed me. I would observe what the others did and try to copy them exactly, but I was never certain that I had it right. I worried about how my ashes looked, whether my sindhur tikka was exactly on my third eye, and if my dhoti hung properly. How much respect should I show, how often, and to whom? The younger babas always seemed to be checking up on me, asking trick questions, trying to unmask me.

On the one hand, I was in the process of un-becoming—

loosening my attachment to whom I thought I was, the objects of my senses, and my perception of the world. And on the other hand, I seemed to be creating a new character for an old story, one that would be believable by a sophisticated audience.

I had been initiated into discipleship, served my gurus, performed my omkars, and practiced my guru mantra. I had been initiated into sannyas and was living with few attachments to the material world. I could meditate for extended periods of time, take cold baths in the winter, fast, sit for hours, days, or weeks doing nothing, and live on no money. I had learned the basic social rules, manners, and etiquette of baba society. Except for my white skin, I looked like a baba, and devotees and common people would touch my feet.

I was practicing—meditating. I would imagine, visualize, as they say, my true self, my inner self, as a shining light, pure emptiness, or pure consciousness (whatever that might be). I would say the word *Kundalini* and imagine that goddess as a serpent, and, with my eyes closed in meditation, see the path she took inside of me as she climbed a path unknown to science, opening the petals of lotuses associated with chakras. And finally, I could imagine her (and therefore myself) joining with supreme consciousness as one thousand petals of a golden lotus blossoming on the top of my head. It was my imagination, and it felt good.

But deep down inside, maybe not so deep, I admitted that I didn't really know.

I felt like an honorary member of an esoteric society, but blood is thicker than water. I couldn't change my foreignness, and I wasn't able to find my place on the grid. I was still using a grid that didn't fit the world I was in.

Sometimes my Hindi was flawless, even elegant; at other times, it was inarticulate and mispronounced. Occasionally, I would speak with great authority to rapt audiences of devotees, espousing ideas that seemed to appear out of nowhere. When this happened it didn't feel as though it was me that was speaking, and this was very puzzling. But then I thought about how a child acquires language. He mimics his parents and his siblings, and by the time he is in school, he is able to make himself understood. Words come from other people's mouths, serving other people's intentions, and we adapt these words and the way they are used to express ourselves in our own way. In this way, I had begun to absorb the words, the expressions, the knowledge of my teachers.

Amar Puri Baba, for reasons I will never know, suspended his disbelief in my ability to learn and began to give me teachings. I wanted him to teach me that very Book of the World of which my departed guru was a master. At first, it seemed that the problem was language itself. My language was based on doing, and the language I was being asked to learn was based on naming. The difference was the focus on nouns instead of verbs. I found everything about naming intimidating—the memorization, the tables, the signs, and the marks.

We soon discovered that the task was formidable because I was illiterate. I had to rely on a newspaper and a watch to know the month, the day, and the time. The sky, which broadcasts every last detail of time and much more, was utterly foreign to me in terms of a language.

What made things more difficult was that his teaching was not organized according to any system I recognized. There were no classes or lessons, nor moments of revelation. It was inseparable from anything else that might be going on around the dhuni. The line between the sacred and the mundane was fuzzy at best. And at those times when it seemed to me he was actually opening up the Book of the World, I found that the sky and the stars had no distinct border with the Earth whose plants and minerals continually spilled into the body, and then emerged as language and speech. I couldn't find where Ayurveda ended and Yoga began, or, for that matter, where our concept of science met with our concept of magic. Everything formed one great stew in which everything lost its individual identity.

I tried to keep notes, but the opportunities for this were rare and I had to wait until I was alone before I could write in my notebook. So I sat and sat and sat and watched and listened. Eventually, I realized that a certain osmosis was taking place. By dint of simply being there and witnessing, knowledge was slowly accumulating on my shelf. And once it was there, it was not only a permanent fixture, but it radiated authority.

Diet became an easy entry into the knowledge of the body and with it Ayurveda, the knowledge of longevity, and also Yoga cosmology. A simple sermon to local villagers when Amar Puri would describe the particular hell worlds their soul might travel to as a result of eating foods such as garlic and onions, or other hells that were reserved for eaters of meat and alcohol, would suddenly become a sublime discourse on the three qualities of nature, called *gunas*; *rajas,* the Active; *tamas,* the Passive; and *sattva,* the Balanced. Not only did these qualities show themselves in food (garlic and onions marked by tamas), but they pervaded creation, and, indeed marked the manifestation of nature herself.

"We babas don't eat tamasic foods because they embody ignorance, laziness, and doubt," Baba said. "Babas don't eat rajasic foods, either, such as anything hot, bitter, sour, dry, or salty, for these are signs of passion of the senses, and a baba marks the absence of passion," he said. "We babas like to eat sattvic foods, whatever is fresh, juicy, light, sweet, and nourishing. These embody balance and harmony with nature. We like milk and ghee, ripe fruits, and fresh tender vegetables, rice, wheat, and honey."

In Amar Puri's world, you were what you ate. It wasn't that you became what you ate, for his rules were descriptive rather than prescriptive or predictive. So a tamasic person would tend to eat tamasic food, a rajasic person rajasic food, and a sattvic person sattvic food.

But then, as I was further instructed, these same three qualities give birth to the great web of illusion, which is the world. I learned that what applies to the cosmos as a whole also applies to its smallest part and therefore also to man. Before the world comes into existence, there is only consciousness. Matter exists in potential, and is indistinguishable from consciousness. Through Amar Puri's guidance, I visualized this as a calm mirrorlike lake, reflecting only itself, which he described as the Cosmic Mind. At this stage, everything is the Same. This is also the potential intellect in man, where discrimination will take place. A single drop, the primordial desire for identity and, therefore, separation, hits the mirror lake, causing ripples, and in this way identity or ego appears as movement, distinguishing it from its background of stillness. The Other is born, and the three qualities of nature, the *gunas,* excite the potential world, the Other, into manifestation.

If there were only sattva, the Balanced, then ego would always be transparent and movement would remain potential. Rajas, the Active, as the agent of the Same, attracts, transforms, and assimilates. Tamas, the Passive, as the agent of the Other, repels and maintains the isolation of things.

The Active, together with the Balanced, attracts matter to consciousness, and produces the five organs of knowledge—smell, taste, sight, touch, and hearing, plus the organizing mind.

These five organs of knowledge perceive and therefore give existence to the five elements of the world: Smell perceives Earth, taste perceives water, sight perceives fire, touch perceives air, and hearing perceives space. The tension between the Active and the Passive shapes the five elements. I could see that the element of space, being the least dense, contains and absorbs the remaining four elements. Here the Active dominates. And at the other extreme, the element of Earth maintains its isolation and shape through its density. This is the pull of the Passive. In the middle, the elements of air, fire, and water reflect the varying degrees of relationship of the Active and the Passive.

"But how can we see these hidden plays of the universe?" I asked Baba. "Because they are marked," said Amar Puri. He explained that the body is covered with marks that not only reflect the celestial vault and the play of heavenly bodies, but also the world and its five elements. He showed me how the play between the Active and the Passive in an individual is apparent on his face. The size and shape of his eyes and other features, the color and texture of his skin and hair, and other marks resemble a written language, from which one can read a story. One can read the story of someone's health, for example, so that if there is a domination of one or more of the five elements, balance can be restored.

Amar Puri Baba taught me how we can also read the sky. "Look," he said just before dawn, pointing to the constellations Orion and Pollux. "Orion is a cradle, with three babes, Brahma, Vishnu, and Shiva. Betelgeuse, the brightest star in that constellation, is a gem and is Anasuya, womanhood personified—the mother of the Lord of Yogis—Dattatreya. Pollux is a house, the ashram of his father, Atri, which is also located high in the snowy Himalayas. Sirius, the brightest star in the sky just below Orion, is Atri, himself. Just near Orion we have Canis Major consisting of four stars, which are Dattatreya's four dogs, marking the four Vedas. Lupus is Dattatreya's cow of plenty, Kamadhenu." Then he read from the sky the story of the birth of Dattatreya as if it were written in an ordinary book.

"One must also know the auspicious and inauspicious times, if not for oneself, then at least so that one may advise others," said Amar Puri. My linear reckonings of time were not compatible with Amar Puri's observation, which seemed more cyclical. Not that the movement of heavenly bodies has a direct effect on the affairs of man, but that man and his story are a reflection of what is written in the sky. And because the heavenly bodies are not inert rocks flying about the universe but divine personalities displaying their strengths and weaknesses, sometimes coming together and sometimes conflicting, celestial events have their reflection or analogy on Earth. With this in mind, Amar Puri said, the wise seek to harmonize their actions with the rest of the universe.

Amar Puri Baba had a Brahmin pandit, Bir Hanuman Shastri Ji, come to teach me Sanskrit every other day for a couple of hours. Because the pandit knew no English, the medium of my study was Hindi. He taught me through memorization. I had no idea what I was memorizing, and the task was simply to repeat what he taught. He would ask me questions, but the only acceptable answers were those I had learned by rote, syllable by syllable.

I longed for some kind of order and began to construct my own tables of the declension of nouns and conjugation of verbs. I felt that without a structure I could not understand what everything meant. Things, after all, seem to have meaning only in relation to other things. I needed a way to visualize the grid upon which this language lived, so I could know what it was that I was learning. But I soon realized that the Sanskrit language was not limited to transparent function, a totality of mechanisms (grammar, syntax, etc.) employed to represent an idea. Nor did words themselves represent ideas. The sounds of words reflected movement in creation. So it wasn't possible to apply the grammatical rules of man to penetrate the secrets of nature.

Amar Puri Baba never sat with me privately, as the pandit did.

The tradition of knowledge is a twenty-four-hour-a-day circus, and people flocked to him all the time for advice, cures, or blessings. He gave me nothing to memorize, nor did he give me instructions or teachings the way I had always imagined great teachers would, but his teaching was continuous. Despite repeated advice from both Hari Puri and Amar Puri to dispense with notetaking, I continued to secretly write notes, and make tables and diagrams, still trying to fit everything I heard into a coherent system. I failed.

One day while I was collecting herbs in the jungle with Kedar Puri Baba, I inadvertently touched some stinging nettles and yelled some expletive. He quickly pulled some leaves from a *krans* plant growing right next to the nettles, and rubbed them on my skin. Within moments, the stinging and burning had vanished.

"Isn't it convenient," I noted, "that nature places the problem and the cure right next to each other?"

"They are always neighbors," Kedar Puri explained. "Everyone knows that!" It dawned on me that their proximity to one meant that there was a relationship between them. Kedar Puri had read the writing of nature's text, made his commentary on it, and I had acquired a tidbit of knowledge. If I had looked where I was putting my hand, I would have seen a plant marked by thousands of barbed spears, and could have translated that as meaning, "Do not touch!" I recognized that in order to read the Book of the World, it is necessary to see how things are marked.

That night Hari Puri Baba appeared to me in a dream, the first time since he had left his body. As in many of my dreams about him, we were sitting on the banks of the Ganga, in what I later realized was Hardwar. He told me that he was in good spirits, and I asked him where he was. He replied that he was in a place I would never think to look for him. "Is this a game?" I asked. He told me that it was indeed a game, and in order to play it, I would require a looking glass. He handed me a mirror with an orange plastic frame, like those you can find in any Indian market, and asked me to look carefully at my face. When I looked into the mirror, my face seemed different, perhaps older. When I turned the mirror at a slight angle, I could see the back of my head as if there were another mirror behind me. When I turned around, I saw myself reflected from every angle. In fact, I was in a room full of mirrors, and there were now thousands of me. The sky had vanished, replaced by a ceiling mirror, and when I looked up, my multitudes looked down on me. Hari Puri was no longer with me, and I was sitting atop an abyss, in a world that consisted only of my own reflected image.

"What a dream!" I said to myself when I woke up. "Freud would have blown a fuse." The dream was so illuminating that even though the sun hadn't yet risen, the world seemed radiant with light. As I walked to the fields and then to the well to take my bath, I could see the phosphorescence of hidden ores shining from beneath the Earth's surface. And I looked up to the sky and saw the same light pouring down from Venus-Shukra as it neared the horizon, where the Earth meets the Sky. I wondered if someone had slipped me a potion during my sleep, because I could see the soft shimmering glows—red, blue, and green—emanating from the stems of plants, spilling their secrets, and connecting them with the firmament.

Plants, minerals, and stars resemble each other, I thought to myself. I sat for my meditation and worship. As I closed my eyes and repeated out loud the fifty-one syllables, the totality of my sounds, and moved in my vocal arc, I found each syllable reflected in the night sky as a star. I became overwhelmed at the resemblances between the syllables' sacred geography in my mouth and that of the stars in the sky: They seemed to occupy the same space, separated by a mirror. But the resemblances didn't stop there.

My own face was like the sky, my two eyes the sun and the moon.

My body was like the Earth, my flesh its soil covering my bones like its rocks and boulders, my veins the great rivers, and my organs the bowels of the Earth, which hides the ores of precious metals. I saw that my ears reflected Space through which sound travels. My breath was the wind, the Air that allows the world to breathe, that I can feel on my skin, touch with my hands. My eyes reflected Fire, my taste Water, and my nose the Earth.

There was something that made things resemble each other. I had spent my life looking for differences, trying to assign an order to all the separate identities based on a scientific grid that contains all our knowledge in the modern West. Now I started to see the world and myself in a new way, a way that linked everything together.

The arrangement of Nature might appear chaotic, but it is not accidental. When I saw that Nature placed two things next to each other, I realized this to be an interior connection between them and that they share a similarity. And in this bond, properties, movements, and influences are exchanged. Syllables and sounds are linked together as they touch and *change* each other. Everything in the world is adjacent to something else, and so is linked into a great chain of the things of the world.

But I also saw how resemblance was not determined by space, how things could resemble and thus influence each other without touching. Things could clone, reflect, or imitate themselves from afar. I remembered how Hari Puri Baba had described how one could reach any point in the universe in less than a second. What was the distance into the mirror that lay between my face and its reflection? What connection made my reflection smile when I smiled? I saw how distant things connected by reflecting each other, dogs barking during the full moon, Mercury transmitting its passions to the man born under the sign of Gemini. Distance between places doesn't exist in this connection, for things reflect each other. And things that connect from a distance are not equal. The stars overwhelm the affairs of man, and the moon the tides.

Then I saw that the chain of the world itself reflected across space. I saw my face in relation to my body as the face of heaven is to space. The relationship among heavenly bodies was reflected in the relationship between me and my world, between people, as well as between and among all things in the world. I felt the rhythmic beat of my pulse reflecting the movement of the moon, the planets and the stars in the sky, and the blood pumping through my veins reflected the great rivers nourishing the Earth, as my blood did my body. I saw my intellect as a microscopic reflection of the Cosmic Mind, and my innermost being as a small flicker of the World Spirit.

I repeated the fifty-one names of the Mother Goddess, producing a necklace of fifty-one syllables that appeared around her swanlike neck, that formed my inner firmament, and that in turn reflected the celestial vault with all its heavenly bodies.

Then I saw a connection in things that was independent of space and mirrors, a power of the Same attracting and pulling all things into itself. Rajas, the Active, excited things into movement and changed them, altering their personalities. It pulled water from the sky to the Earth, and pulled water from the Earth into the sky. It pulled the roots of plants into the soil toward the water that it pulled from the sky. It pulled sacrifices into the fire and the smoke of the burnt offerings to the heavens where they could be enjoyed by the gods. It had the power of making things identical to each other. It had pulled me to India, and then to yogis, and to Hari Puri Baba. It had pulled me into a new lifestyle, and now a new way of thinking.

Left unchecked, the Active, like a great fire, would consume everything in the world and make it into a homogeneous mass, like the pure ashes of a dhuni. But this doesn't happen because its opposite, the Passive, is always present in the form of inertia, identity, and separation, therefore resisting the Active.

The language that I was being taught established a network from one end of the universe to the other. I learned to recognize the *brahmi* plant by the resemblance of the twin hemispheres of its leaf to the human brain, that indicates its influence over brain functions, and that the plant's effects are enhanced by combining it with the meat of the almond or walnut, both of which resemble the soft human brain protected by the hard human skull. And that the shells of these nuts treat skull injury. How else could I recognize ginseng, if not for the shape of the root resembling the human body, informing me of its tonic properties? I could now know that the brahmi plant was cooling, like the Moon, for its taste is bitter. All these plants spoke a silent language to those who knew it, revealing the secrets of their stems, leaves, and roots. Nature is filled with marks and flags that may capture our perception and point us toward a hidden connection.

"Am I sure I am me?" I asked myself, feeling very different now that I was seeing the universe with new eyes. I didn't dare look at myself in a mirror, but I did examine my hands and feet to make sure they were still mine, because I felt like someone else.

17

Possession

Dungri Hill rises straight up nine hundred feet from the floor of the brush plain amid the ancient Arravalli Hills in northern Rajasthan. It was a rocky edifice with no signs of human habitation or activity but it *wasn't* inert rock. For those who knew, and they were very few, it possessed a personality. Wasn't Dungri Hill Shiva's signature and, indeed, the god, himself? Didn't that call into play hidden things? Not the ores buried in the rock but spirit buried in matter. Wasn't it as clear then, as it is now?

Hira Lal, who lived in a small village nearby, had never heard of Dungri Hill. He had never been more than a mile from home. An illiterate fourteen-year-old who had never been to school, Hira Lal spent his days tending his family's goats. His days were an endless repetition of taking his goats to graze in the same grassless spot on the edge of the forest. He would sleep through the day, and dream shapeless unpopulated dreams. He spoke very little as he had nothing to say. But he was a voyeur; he liked to observe unobserved.

One day, during the season when mangoes were just starting to ripen, Hira Lal spread his ragged cloth on the ground and settled in for his daily siesta in the shade of a great ashoka tree. Looking up into the lower branches, he saw a green parrot unlike any bird he

had ever seen before. Its wings and tail were tipped with gold and
it had a red crown. To his great delight, it flew out of the tree and
landed beside him.

Hira Lal pounced on the poor bird, trying to capture it, but it
flew into a bush some dozen paces away. He was so enchanted by
the bird that he forgot about his goats and followed it into the jungle until he reached a large stream and realized that he was lost. He
walked around in great circles arriving time and again at the stream,
and then he sniffed the faint smell of smoke. Following his nose, he
came to a clearing where there was a small hillock, boulders, and a
cave. A thin plume of smoke rose from the cave and Hira Lal crept
closer and concealed himself in the brush.

He could make out a strange being sitting at the entrance of
the cave, a naked old man with gnarled vines of dreadlocks that
merged with the earth. Hira Lal imagined that this must be the god,
Kubera, Lord of the Earth Spirits, guarding the cave that contained
the riches and treasures of the earth. His instinct told him to run
away, but his curiosity got the better of him, and he inched closer to
what he now realized was an old baba, but who looked like a small
banyan tree. Jungle orchids grew out of his matted hair.

Eventually the gaze of the baba fell upon him. The baba's eyes
grew wide as full moons, and anger seemed to fill his body when
he saw Hira Lal observing him. "*I* am the observer, you little sister-
fucker!" he shouted.

All of Hira Lal's meek mental circuits snapped, he turned and
ran, and didn't stop until night had fallen. His animal instinct must
have brought him back to his village the following day, for by then,
the rest of his brain seemed to have burnt to a crisp. His expression
was blank as the sky was cloudless, and he couldn't speak, eat, or
drink, but each time a storm was in the air, the boy would thrash
about on the ground. His family thought that he had been possessed

by a ghost, and they tethered him with a thick hemp rope. They called in exorcists who caused his aunts to fall into a trance, but the boy himself just lay there. The exorcists danced, throwing offerings into the fire, and shouted louder into the spirit world, but there was no response. Then his family summoned healers who took his pulse, examined his tongue, and looked in his eyes, but his health was that of a young bull.

One day, about two weeks after Hira Lal had been stricken, while he was thrashing about on the ground, he began to yell, "Take these bonds off of me! Take them off at once!"

Not only was he speaking, but the piddly squeaky mumbling was gone. His voice was loud, passionate, and full of authority. "We can't take off the bonds, child, they are for your own protection," his family replied.

"Idiots!" roared the boy. "What are you protecting me from? Nothing can harm me. Take these off at once."

Now everyone became very frightened, and they touched their ear lobes twice. "No wonder our local exorcists couldn't find anything," Hira Lal's father cried. "There must be some really powerful evil spirit in there!" The old village priest stepped forward and called out, "Who are you in there?"

"Ah! So there is someone who understands that perhaps I am not who you think I am! Still, you are all idiots!" said Hira Lal. The boy then explained to them that Hira Lal was gone and would never return. He agreed not to hurt anyone and said he would reveal his identity once the ropes were removed and a chair was brought for him. He refused to sit on the ground with everyone else.

He told them that his name was Baba Jai Ram Puri and that he had been wandering in the forest for at least a couple of hundred years. The priest refused to be convinced without some display of power but immediately regretted his demand, when the torrent of Vedic mantras that came rushing out of Hira Lal's mouth caused the earth to tremble and the birds to fly out of their nests. Then Hira Lal swore at the priest in Sanskrit, using language so foul as to cause the earth to belch sulfur fumes.

"You want *chamak,* flash? Take me to Dungri Mahadev!" he demanded. The Dungri Hill? Why? "Call Amar Puri Baba and Phul Puri Baba," he demanded. "One hundred thousand people will come to greet me!"

When I returned to Amloda Kund after seven years, I felt strongly that I had completed a circle. For one thing, I felt I had "arrived," that at last I "belonged." By then there were newer babas. I had become one of the older guru bhais, and I could see my younger brothers going through what I had gone through. I was not the only one who sniffed the winds and sensed that this was the moment to be with Amar Puri, revisit old times, and catch up on what everyone was doing. Kalyan Puri Baba arrived from Omkareshwar, Darshan Giri Baba from Kundel Gufa near Indore, Silverbeard Raghunath Puri Baba from Kanpur, as well as several more local sadhus. Somehow they all knew something hidden was about to be revealed.

I was now reading the Book of the World, not fluently but well enough to give me great pleasure. It was not unlike the small pleasure I experienced at being able to read the Hindi billboards, such as the Coca Cola's, *"da ree-al ting."* I saw Amloda with very different eyes from before. I was no longer concerned with what things meant, the magical spring, the dhuni, the tree of spirits, nor what their purpose was. Now I focused on their grammar, syntax, and commentary. I would look down at my hands, wondering if they were mine. Was I still me? I didn't think so.

It made a great deal of sense that the lanky Phul Puri, who was the Mahant of Udaypuria and around the same age as Amar Puri, arrived on a Wednesday, Mercury-day, to solve the mystery of our gathering. "Seems there's this young boy who claims to be Jai Ram Puri Baba, our very own Jai Ram Puri Baba from Udaypuria!"

"Which Jai Ram Puri?" asked Amar Puri Baba.

"The old man," replied Phul Puri, "the guru of Udaypuri Baba who built Udaypuria hundreds of years ago."

"Slow down," said Amar Puri, nobody's fool. He extracted his astrological almanac from beneath his tiger skin. "What makes you believe the boy is the old man? A perfected yogi like yourself?" he sneered as he leafed through the pages.

"It was the message he sent me," said Phul Puri, as he tied his white wispy beard into a knot under his chin, "He wrote, 'You see, your building of rock and limestone is crumbling, and yet my body is in the full bloom of youth.' Hundreds of years ago, when Uday Puri Baba and Jai Ram Puri Baba, chela and guru, roamed through Rajasthan, they came to this spring, and settled there for some years. Uday Puri Baba liked the spot so much that he built an ashram there. However, when the work was complete, Jai Ram Puri Baba announced his departure, and he cursed his disciple, saying that his ashram would end up in the middle of a noisy bazaar, and that Jai Ram Puri's body would last longer than Uday Puri's buildings. Then he went to Dungri Hill, which he always called Dungri Mahadev, the great god Dungri. There have never been any reports of his death, but there have been stories that he was still roaming about.

"He has sent you and me an invitation to appear at a feast at the top of Dungri Hill," continued Phul Puri, "and I've come to take you there."

As Jai Ram Puri had predicted, more than a hundred thousand people swarmed to greet him. They came by bus, bullock cart, jitney, car, rickshaw, and scooter, but the vast majority walked.

From above it looked as though the Shiva linga had been adorned with flowers of every hue. The faithful had come to welcome back the Old Baba.

The road stopped considerably short of the hill. A small crowd surged around our two jeeps, into which we had managed to fit seventeen sadhus. We walked through the great multitude, with people touching our feet, some giving each of us a couple of coins as dakshina. Hundreds followed us in the scorching sun, cheering us on with slogans. Many of our devotees showed up as well, and we were joined by a man with long unkempt hair and a dirty lungi.

"Come on," he said in a familiar voice with an almost British accent acquired at the Sindia School in Gwalior, "You don't recognize me?" I squinted at him and scratched my beard. "You squint your eyes just like your guru," he said. Then I realized that it was Dr. Rathor.

Rathor told me that he had left the medical profession to become a baba. "It was the only thing I could do," he explained. He had been very impressed with Hari Puri Baba. "You realize that he was brain-dead, don't you?"

Amar Puri Baba gave me eleven rupees. "You watch me, son, if I give the signal that the boy is really Baba Jai Ram Puri, then you give him this dakshina," he said.

"What do you think, Baba Ji?" I asked him.

"The signs are all there, but who knows until we see him," he replied.

Kedar Puri tugged at my arm. "Give me some money for dakshina, Ram Puri, I don't have any." I found two five-rupee notes and a one-rupee coin in my bag-of-wishes and gave them to my guru brother.

"I knew that he was conscious that whole time," continued Dr. Rathor, "but it didn't make sense to me. That wasn't all. Do you have any idea how many patients under my care with terminal TB walked out of the hospital under their own steam? I got all the credit, and they were calling me the doctor of miracles. Then Hari Puri Baba started appearing in my dreams and told me not to worry. Gradually all my knowledge started to seem insignificant. I couldn't heal these poor people. I could only do what I was trained to do and watch them die. I was powerless, yet an old brain-dead baba could heal them! By the time he reentered his body, I knew that I had come in contact with a siddha, a realized being. I watched my years of training and practice crumble like a building made out of adulterated cement. The day before he left the hospital, I asked him for his mantra. He told me that I was too late; he wasn't making disciples any more. So I want to become your disciple."

"What?" I exclaimed. "You are out of your mind." He laughed like a mad man. "I'm a foreigner, an outsider to this tradition," I said. "Besides, there are babas like Amar Puri, Phul Puri, and so many other sadhus, with great powers and understanding and wisdom. Become one of their disciples."

"Even Hari Puri suggested that at first."

"So why don't you follow his advice?"

"Because it's his mantra I want, and I told him that, and he told me that if that was the case, then I'd have to get it from either you or Kedar Puri Baba."

"I'll be your guru," said Kedar Puri Baba, beating his chest.

"Then he told me to wait until his body was buried and there was a *murti,* a statue in his likeness, and a Shiva linga on top of his grave. Afterward, to give it a little time and find Ram Puri who would give it to me."

"There's just no way," I said. "I can't do it. Find a real Indian baba."

"Why not let me. . . ." Kedar Puri interrupted.

"Stop it, guru bhai!" I said.

At the top, a large colorful awning had been set up; rugs had been laid down, with cushions and pillows, and a single chair for the boy Hira Lal. Others were sitting around him, including several officials, senior police officers, and a few of the privileged, including the priest from the village, who was by now a celebrity. But they all stood up and moved back as our troop of babas and followers arrived. I looked at the boy, and he seemed so small and insignificant. How could this be the great baba? I thought.

Kedar Puri continued to nag me, pulling at my arm. "We'll make five gurus, Ram Puri. You will give the mantra, I'll give the rudraksha, and for the other three, well there are many sadhus to choose from."

"I said no!" I was becoming angry with him and something else I couldn't put my finger on was upsetting me.

Hira Lal yelled out

om namo narayan!

What a voice! I thought, amazed that it could come from such a puny body. He called Amar Puri and Phul Puri by name, and spoke to them in a gruff manner using the informal honorific address—he spoke down to them. They were the most senior Naga sannyasis in this part of India, but he addressed them as children. I was hardly able to believe my eyes as Amar Puri and Phul Puri, who bowed down to no human authority, approached the boy with their hands together, and knelt in front of him, touching their foreheads to his feet.

"The young boy is possessed," said Rathor. "It's the baba, Baba Jai Ram Puri, calling the shots, like a puppeteer."

I was frightened, as though I was standing on a high precipice overlooking an abyss. All the babas were prostrating themselves before the boy. I didn't want to get too close to the edge until I had to. Avoid eye contact, I said to myself, but listen to his words.

He rattled off the names of babas that had been dead for hundreds of years, as if they were among the crowd. He spoke of Parshuram Puri Baba and Uday Puri Baba. Turning to Amar Puri he told him that he knew his guru, Daryal Puri Baba. "A rascal," he said. "I was with Sandhya Puri Baba when he arrived in Datt Akhara from Omkareshwar with his guru bhai Pagal Puri fifty-four years ago. Shiv Dayal Puri Baba was Pir, then. And you, Kalyan Puri Baba, I saw you arrive in Datt Akhara thirty-four years ago. You were a kid, then," the boy said.

Then I remembered the eleven rupees in my hand. Everyone else had already given their dakshina, but I decided to wait for the right moment. I could feel Kedar Puri's body heat on my right.

Hira Lal instructed Phul Puri to initiate him in the name of Jai Ram Puri with the Sacrament of the Five Gurus so that Jai Ram Puri would be the boy's main guru and the boy would henceforth be known as Hira Puri Baba. He asked Amar Puri to be among the Five and give him the rudraksha, the sign of discipleship.

Noticing the dakshina in my hand, Kedar Puri pushed me forward. Hira Lal's gaze met my eyes. I couldn't unlock our visual connection and felt disoriented and disturbed.

"But you're a white boy!" said the new Hira Puri Baba, "and yet. . . ." His eyes widened as he looked inside me, through my captive eyes, then laughed, and turned away. What the hell did he see? I wondered.

Kedar Puri led me away. "Ram Puri, you have to take me more seriously."

"You're giving me a big pain in my head, Kedar Puri!" I said to him, disentangling myself.

"He could have gone inside me, you know," said Kedar Puri Baba. "He only entered you because he wants to see Am-rika."

"What? Who?" I was shocked.

"You haven't been listening to anything I've been saying!" he said. "Guru Ji! Hari Puri Baba, of course!"

This was a blow from below the belt. It all came at me at once with the force of a thousand elephants.

"No, not the Am-rika thing, the possession thing!" I responded. He must have assumed that I knew, as everyone else did, that I too was possessed.

I didn't need his answer, and I wouldn't have heard it even if he had opened his mouth, for my ears buzzed and blood was rushing to my head. I felt like slapping him in the face, but that would have been killing the messenger. My knees buckled, I had an empty feeling in my stomach, and the world started to spin. I was possessed! Hari Puri was inside me.

That was why some disciples began to act like their dead gurus. That was why sometimes when I spoke I didn't know where the thoughts and words came from. That was why I had acquired Hari Puri's voice. In order to say *his* words.

But, surely I was jumping to conclusions? I needed confirmation that this was true, just as the boy on the chair had demanded it. I tried to get Amar Puri's attention, or even Darshan Giri's, Kalyan Puri's, or Silverbeard's, but they were somewhere in the seventeenth century with the Old Baba. I was assaulted by a river of disturbing thoughts when I realized that everyone else had known this all along. Was I so far outside, even among outsiders? I wondered what, if anything, I had learned in all those years. Was my body-mind just a shell for spirits to enter and live, like parasites?

It all became crystal clear to me, at that moment of madness. *They* were the enemy. Amar Puri, Kedar Puri, and all the rest were co-conspirators, pulling the wool over my eyes, tricking me, and laughing behind my back. The stupid white kid. I'd had enough, this had gone too far. I had to leave.

I pushed poor Dr. Rathor out of the way as I struggled through the crowd. Kedar Puri couldn't understand my shock and anger, but he knew not to follow me. I stormed blindly down the hill, my thoughts drowning out the din of the mela, the loudspeakers, and the drummers and musicians singing praises of the Great God.

"Are my thoughts and ideas really mine?" I shouted. How could I tell which were mine and which Hari Puri's? Were all ideas like spirits living in the body-mind of human shells? I identify myself with thoughts I believe I create, but perhaps those aren't really mine. Maybe I don't own them as a kind of intellectual property. Perhaps they are non-ownable and non-corporeal beings.

My pace quickened as the crowd thinned, but I had gone in the wrong direction, and I ended up in the jungle, leaping over bushes, fallen trees, and small boulders. I felt that I had to get away as fast as possible but from what and to what? Then night fell.

I felt violated. This was not consensual possession. Shouldn't he have asked me first? When had he actually entered me? When my attention had been diverted, that's when it always happens. He couldn't have done it while he was still alive. Perhaps he never really died? No, no, that wasn't possible, there were too many witnesses.

The darkness slowly spread its blanket over the dense foliage, but I was oblivious to it. I went carefully over the five years since Hari Puri Baba's samadhi. I had meditated in front of his tomb and statue every day for several years. I had had so many conversations with him and dreams of him. He must have been inside me all that time. What were the signs? The pain when I had hit my coccyx. That was it. I could still feel it. The bastard. So, now there were two of us. Okay, I thought, *you* lead me through this jungle, I'm switching off.

It seemed to be me, however, that I ran out of gas, and fell to the ground. I gathered some leaves into a pile and spread my dhoti over it. Mosquitoes feasted on the rare blood of a naked white man. "Maybe I should just sit here forever, without moving, and let Guru Ji keep my body alive!" I mused.

The thoughts persisted. "Did I cut a deal for my soul in return for knowledge? When could that have happened? Ah, taking guru mantra! Or was it the knowledge sacrament of sannyas? Hari Puri had said in the initiation of the Five Gurus in which he gave me guru mantra that he was only a witness of Guru Dattatreya. Was Guru Dattatreya my Mephistopheles? Stop this!" I commanded myself.

I tried meditating, watching the thoughts run by, but, like wild vines in the monsoon, they grew fatter and more numerous, and became entangled with each other. Do I need an exorcist? I wondered. Hari Puri Baba would laugh at him, and besides, I could never throw him out, just like that! And why had no one told me? Maybe I was never meant to find out? After all, what difference did it make? But there *was* a big difference. I no longer knew who was thinking things in my head and who was saying what came out of my mouth.

Sitting there in the dark, I realized I was not alone. I knew crows were there, nodding in the trees, trying to stay awake, so they could make their reports. But surely it wasn't me who knew that but him. I could hear the movements of monkeys in the branches above and the owls tormented me with their "Who? Who? Who?" There were also two demons that I had come to know in Kashi, the henchmen of the fearful god, Mahakal Bhairon, one of the manifestations of Shiva. Their simple but ancient names were Doubt and Confusion. Was I guilty of the sin of killing a Brahmin, like Mahakal Bhairon, who sliced off the fifth head of the Creator God Brahma, the first

Brahmin? Was I condemned to carry his skull welded to my hand, as he did, begging for my subsistence till my sin was expiated? To all the holy places for twelve cosmic years, the cycle of cosmic Jupiter-Guru, whose mark was on my face? Or did I carry only his spirit?

I longed to root into the forest soil and merge. But Doubt hounded me like Bhairon's black dog and Dattatreya's Four. I could hear them yelping in the distance. "What do babas do?" I asked myself. "Nothing," I replied, "they just hang out."

"Keep moving!" commanded Doubt, whose fine-featured youthful face contradicted his authority.

"Leave this place!" commanded Confusion whose face was hidden by a fog. "Go back to Am-rika!" he shouted. "You'll be safe there."

"You don't belong here," Doubt agreed. "What have they taught you, these great gurus of yours? Are you free? Liberated? Rich? Or do you have a baba on your back? What have you accomplished other than breaking the connection with the source of your own existence? You have failed miserably."

"I've learned a lot!" I retorted.

"Such as . . ." asked Confusion.

"I've learned how nature and the world are connected in unfolding illusion, and how its marks and signatures reveal its hidden nature," I boasted.

"Even," suggested Confusion, "if this had the slightest relevance in this modern world of jumbo jets, which personally, I doubt, let me ask you the big question: Is this you talking or him? Whose knowledge, kid, yours or his?"

Confusion had a point, there, one I couldn't refute. It wasn't me talking, and it wasn't my knowledge.

"You didn't even put up much of a fight," said Doubt. "You

must go now, and we too must leave before the first rays of the sun appear. We prefer night."

The following morning, there was no path hewn through the jungle for me as there had appeared to be the day before, and I spent half the day threading myself through the underbrush until I reached a pasture. There a young goatherd, about the same age as Hira Lal, offered to guide me to the road. When I looked down at my hands, I saw that I was still clutching eleven rupees. I gave the young boy his dakshina.

18

Deconstruction

"Where you going?" asked the rickshaw wala, keeping pace with me on his three-wheeler. A heavy haze of dust hung over Jaipur sealing in the summer heat. Cold *lassi* vendors were doing a brisk business. "Get in," he said, "I'll take you wherever you're going."

The wind felt good on my bare chest when the rickshaw wala started pedaling down the wide avenues. I never gave him a destination, but he seemed to know where he was going. "I have no money to give you," I said, hoping he wouldn't stop. "No matter," he replied. "You foreign baba, no?"

He could have meant anything by *baba,* but when he joined those incongruous sounds, *for-in* and *baba,* a location arose in his consciousness, the Shiva Hotel. Not exactly an ashram, and having little to do with the Great God, it was more of a hippie crash-pad cum occasional opium den, a somewhat rebuilt *haveli* in incredibly bad taste, before havelis became the rage. In the well-kept garden was a café, filled with foreign seekers, adventurers, and back-packers.

Once the rickshaw wala had deposited me there, I didn't notice him depart. Must have been one of Hari Puri's allies from the spirit world, I thought. He did read my mind, however. This time I knew it was *my* mind I was talking about because I had been longing for a familiar landscape and the Shiva Hotel was about as close as it got.

As it was sunset, a few foreign couples strolled in the garden watching the sky haze turn ozone orange and then purple. They seemed as foreign to me as I must have looked to them. I was bare to the waist, my dhoti torn in places from my war with brambles, and my feet looking as though I had just walked there from Siberia.

I sat down at one of the tables to consider my next move and checked my bag-of-wishes for any hidden coins. "Let there be something there," I said under my breath as I saw a smiling waiter in an ill-fitting uniform approach my table. What am I saying? I thought. *He* gave me the bag, *he* should make sure something's there! How much is tea in a place like this? I found a soiled five-rupee note. Had it been there before? If it had, I should have given it to the rickshaw wala.

Then I heard a familiar voice, with an accent I could never forget, coming from behind me. I listened intently. "The ice palace . . ." I heard him say. I walked around the table at which he was sitting with a British couple. I must have been staring. He looked different. "Yes?" he questioned, smiling, "Baba?" He had always spoken very politely.

"The boat," I said. "The boat?" he asked. "You know, the ferry from Karachi to Bombay?" I fumbled my words. "What, seven years ago, maybe eight?" It had to be him.

"Of course, you're the American. Oh my god, so good to meet you again!" he said, standing up. "And I see you've gone, uh, native?" he laughed and hugged me. "Don't tell me you're still here?" His smile was infectious.

If I had seen him on the street, I would have walked right past him. Gone were the long black locks, the D'Artagnan moustache, the flamboyant orange gown, and the Aladdin slippers. Cartouche now looked like a gypsy about to sell me a second-hand automobile. His hair was greased back, his mustache looked as if it were carefully drawn just above his upper lip with a fine camelhair brush, he wore a colorful polyester shirt and pants, and patent leather shoes.

"Not on the baba trip anymore?" I asked him.

"Buying crystals," Cartouche said. "Cheap here in Jaipur, good market in London. Crystal healing's the rage, now," he explained. "What, with all the gurus and yoga and everything." The exaggerated French accent was now toned down, and I could hear the influence of London. His eyes darted around, not looking directly at me but examining me carefully.

"Does it work?" I asked him.

"They think it does," he replied and invited me to move in with him for a few days while he completed his shopping for stones.

Even though I had known Cartouche for less than twenty-four hours more than seven years earlier, I felt a strong kinship with him. Of all the people I knew in the world, I couldn't have thought of a better person to run into. In fact, it was only at this moment that I realized just how much influence this man had had on my life. I had unwittingly tried to emulate him—not his thoughts, tastes, or habits, all of which were unknown to me, but his persona, or rather my projection of it. During these years, I had built a relationship with a man that didn't exist outside of my thoughts. And here he was, so different from my imagination.

"So why did you leave the baba trip?" I asked him, feeling that somehow he had betrayed me.

"I'm not into austerities," he said. "I like wine, women, and song, I guess. Being a baba was a great experience, but I have other things to do." A smile spread across his face.

I had taken him very seriously that night on the ship crossing the Arabian Sea. His notes in my notebook were the foundation on which I built my life among sadhus. I thought of what my mother had said about Dr. Spock not being the only child psychologist telling parents how to raise their children in the fifties. She had attended several lectures by another expert in childrearing, and read his book. She had been so impressed with his knowledge and under-standing of children that she applied all his theories to me. Then he had disappeared: no more lectures or books. Many years later, when I was already an adult, she ran into this doctor at a cocktail party. She asked him why he hadn't continued, as Dr. Spock had done. He replied that he had discovered that his theories just didn't work and so he became a stockbroker.

Since Cartouche had a memory like a hard drive, when I brought up that night on the ship, he remembered much more than I could recall; my embroidered shoulder bag as well as my prize chillam from Afghanistan, inlaid with colored glass that looked like gems. Both items were long gone, from my possession as well as my memory.

He was impressed when he heard my Hindi and even more when I spoke to him at length about the past seven years. I told him all about Hari Puri, my time with Amar Puri, the other babas I had met, and the teachings. My stories delighted him, and he told me that I had taken this baba thing considerably further than he had.

"Why did you send me to Hari Puri Baba?" I asked him.

"I gave you a list five pages long," said Cartouche as he placed a wooden box full of different stones on his bed. "You made all the choices."

"Give me a break, Cartouche," I snapped. "You know that's not the case. There's never been any doubt in my mind that you sent me to him. Maybe not in so many words, but it was clear from the way you spoke of him. You knew I would go to him."

"Hold on, Ram Puri," he stopped me. It was the first time he had pronounced my seven-year-old name. He sat down on the bed next to his treasure chest of crystals and looked into my eyes. "Is there a problem?" he asked, showing genuine concern. "You seem to be the luckiest man in the world. Still, I hear something in your voice."

"There's no problem," I lied. "I just want you to know how much influence you can have over someone. Did you know who these people were that you sent me to?" I asked.

"Would you have preferred me to send you to some ordinary people?" he replied.

"That's not the point," I said. "Don't you consider what you did a bit, shall we say, reckless?"

"We are both reckless people, Ram Puri, you could have easily found a guru in Muktananda or even Maharishi Mahesh Yogi, but I knew that that just wouldn't cut it for you."

"I mean, I just wasn't ready for what I walked into," I said. "Do you really understand what's involved, here, what the tradition of knowledge is really all about?"

Cartouche smiled again and lit a cigarette. He offered me one, but I told him that I didn't smoke cigarettes. "Did you think of the tradition of knowledge as a hobby? Did you think that the nectar of immortality was attainable without surrendering body, mind, and resources?"

"Words, Cartouche, those are just words!" I said.

"Correct, my dear Ram Puri, they may be just words," said Cartouche, "for look what words have become for us. They are no longer signs of the correspondences of the world, but are the property of man's arbitrary and rational opinions. And we use these words, now, as part of a network of Western man's current yet fickle ideas whose very existence is contrary to the tradition of knowledge."

"Of course, but there is a whole other side to this, which is putting in doubt everything I've learned," I said.

"Yes, and that is . . . ?" he asked.

"Cartouche, I'm possessed," I said in a hushed voice.

He burst out laughing. "I could have told you that. Possessed and passionate. You look like a zombie!" he commented.

"It's not funny," I said. "I'm possessed by Hari Puri Baba's ghost!"

"Then we have another thing in common," said Cartouche, dismissive of my major revelation. "I am also possessed!" he said. "I'm possessed by the ghost of Paracelsus!"

"Who?" I asked, beginning to lose my patience.

"I have in me the sixteenth-century German, or at least what we now call German, alchemist, or what we now call alchemist," he said. "I believe you and I were acquainted in the sixteenth century, and we were both cursed, me, never to forget who I am, you, not to remember who you are."

Now I knew he was out of his mind. However, what he then told me changed everything.

"You're possessed by a lot more than Hari Puri Baba, my brother," he said. "You are possessed by a spirit so powerful that it determines the way you see the world, relate to it, think, and speak. It puts the very ideas you have in your head, and provides you with the words that fall out of your mouth. You are possessed by, how shall I call it . . . ah, your Western Mind. You weren't aware of this?" he asked, scratching his head.

"I've left the West, Cartouche, this is the first time in years that I've even spoken English," I said.

"But you could also renounce India forever, live in the West, and you would still be possessed by Hari Puri. Powerful spirits are able to take us over in all kinds of ways and use us for their own purposes. Your way of looking at the world is not really yours at all. It belongs to the great spirit of the West."

"But, my thinking is no longer Western. I now believe in magic, reincarnation, and ghosts!" I said.

"Don't get me wrong," said Cartouche, "I never said that you're possessed *only* by Western discourse. It's dominant, but still it is competing for space with Hari Puri Baba and God knows what or who else. It's just that you somehow take it for granted that this way of seeing and understanding the world is you and that everything else is alien."

I thought back to one of my initial reactions to my possession: I seemed to be a host organism for all sorts of bodiless consciousnesses. Perhaps the most powerful of the ghosts can be always identified as whatever feels normal, my thoughts, ideas, feelings, and taste—the Same.

"And even with Hari Puri Baba inside you, what you believe to be your normal self is working overtime to convert all the baba's precious knowledge into another format," he said. "And then you suddenly think you've sold your soul to the devil, the ultimate Other." He started laughing.

"What's so funny this time?" I asked.

"It's just that you think you've made a deal with Mephistopheles, you've swapped yourself for knowledge, and yet you degrade the knowledge by reformatting it and trying to maintain your previous allegiance. That's no way to do business!"

I had to laugh as well.

"But, listen," he continued. "We're also talking of a man's ghost who enters another body because he wants something from that body and its mind."

Like the heavens filled with sparkles he knows
The stars shine within him; the world is prose.

Cartouche sang, paraphrasing the alchemist Paracelsus. "The sage reflects and envelops the world in which he finds himself," Cartouche said, and emptied his box of stones onto the bed and began to sort them—big ones, little ones, special ones, ordinary ones.

"Around the beginning of the seventeenth century, a particularly hungry spirit foraging the meat of the thinking of the intellectual class, reached critical mass, and spread its consciousness over all of Europe. Language, as it was known and practiced, ceased to exist. Thinking, speaking, writing, all expression changed. The way of knowing changed. Descartes taught us Europeans that mathematics, algebra, is the language of God that he used to create and maintain the world, and eventually this became the idea that truth lies only within the realm of human reason. And they call this period the Enlightenment, the Age of Reason."

"Unbelievable," I said. "It seems backward, somehow!"

"Language and the World became disconnected. Language began to express man's ideas about the world rather than being an articulation of the world itself," said Cartouche comparing two long rose pink crystals. One went in the special pile, one in the ordinary.

"A new mapping process began. Words got lost, they no longer marked anything and were condemned to live only on the pages of books, from which they were borrowed to populate people's speech."

Cartouche pulled an olive green duffle bag and a briefcase from under the bed. He wrapped the extraordinary rose pink crystal in wax paper and then a little plastic Ziplock bag. Ziplocks were more rare than rose crystals in India at that time.

"Things became nothing more than the sum of their component parts. Those who saw connections between things based on resemblances were thought of as visionaries or madmen because magic lost its authority and was placed in the storage bin of the curious but false. Sages like Hari Puri Baba, who read nature and books as a single text, were expelled to the margins of society and also stripped of their authority. You see, similarities no longer mattered. Differences became important. This great spirit bloated with gray matter sprung a million legs and began to refashion the world by placing it in an order that was a negotiation between algebra and the fickle opinions of man, based on his so-called rational mind. Castrated words became the components of knowledge."

"Wow," I gasped, "you certainly don't hold the West in high regard, Cartouche."

"I'm not making a moral judgment here," he replied. "It's not about good and evil, better or worse. It's about witnessing, and therefore seeing.

The Great Shadow ate Language with relish

sang Cartouche in a funny British accent. "Like an anteater, he sucked it out from where it hid in the mystery of the mark, and left both the mark and Language empty. He granted Language only function, like a machine, but no other existence," he said.

I knew what he said was right from my study of Sanskrit. It was one of the early dilemmas I had had to contend with.

"Language was emptied of all content. All that remains is representation," said Cartouche. "Text ceased to exist, as well as it's Commentary, *so that it may be known,* and Language went from the safekeeping of knowers, from the safekeeping of oral traditions, to the ownership of a rational elite. The very existence of Language now depended on its rational analysis. Replacing commentary, criticism became the criterion of a statement's precision, appropriateness, or expressive value."

"But that's the West and this is the East, and 'ne'er the twain shall meet.' Readers of the World still exist here, and the tradition is still alive and vibrant," I said. "I know. I've seen it with my own eyes."

"Don't fool yourself. You happened to be lucky and stumbled upon some astounding ghosts. But their numbers are dwindling. Remember that the nature of this Great Shadow of the West is that men possessed by it are driven to map the entire universe, and that includes India. In India, the Tradition is the subject of knowledge not its object. From a Western viewpoint, however, it is represented by something else. So when you came to India, you lent your body and your mind to this mapping enterprise. It doesn't matter that you were thrown pearls. You chopped them up, like a good little zombie, mixed them with a healthy dose of imagination, and produced a fascinating board game about resemblance and illusion."

"C'mon, Cartouche, I've always dropped my preconceived Western notions, and kept an open mind on everything," I protested.

"You can leave the West, but it doesn't leave you. This so-called open mind you're speaking of has no interest in mapping, in representing? Your greatest illusion is that you have an open mind and free choice."

I thought about this. It's something we rarely question in the West. We have a well-established tradition about the superiority of the Western way of understanding the world. But from the Indian point of view, these guys suddenly come along in the nineteenth century and reorder and redefine everything that wise men have known for thousands of years.

Cartouche finished putting all the bigger stones into his duffle bag, and started to examine the smaller ones before wrapping them up and placing them in his briefcase. "So, just how does the West represent and construct India?"

"I'm all ears," I said.

"The first thing to understand is that the West is the Same and India is the Other, the West is normal and India is abnormal. The West is rational, India is irrational, the West is active, India is passive. The problem arises when the West tries to fit the large round pegs of India into its small square holes. For this it needs to be reformatted, its categories altered, and its elements be universalized. This is the foundation of Imperial Knowledge. The first step is to give a bit of order to the chaos of Indian culture, which is made possible by essentializing India. But, of course, essences don't really exist. Once we have a grid, the Table of All Things, we want to know where exactly each thing can be found on it. How about religion? What is the religion of India?" Cartouche asked.

"Hinduism, of course," I answered.

"Yeh, yeh, well . . ." he mumbled, "what do we Europeans know about religion? Christianity, Judaism, and Islam are familiar to us. Two attributes they share jump out right away: a central, sacred text, which represents authority in all its manifestations, and a central doctrine that gives an order to thinking. When the British came to India, they tried to locate the native religion on their grid, by searching for the essences of text and doctrine. The *Bhagavad Gita* became the prime candidate for text, and Advaita Vedanta, thought of as sort of an exegesis of the *Gita,* was reduced to a simple form to serve as the central doctrine."

"How is that possible?" I asked. "There are so many different beliefs, myths, rituals, and laws, and there are innumerable texts and strong literary traditions."

"Yes, indeed. The same text sometimes had many different versions, some even contradictory. If the culture and religion of the Indians were to be studied, then in post-Enlightenment thinking, books had to be read and discussed so that the consensus could be fitted comfortably on the grid. We see other cultures through the lens of our own. What other access did colonial administrators and Christian missionaries have to understand Indian culture? We Europeans learn by reading. Now, of course, we have television. The video screen is just a further extension of Gutenberg.

"Because there was no standardization among Indian texts, the first work of academics was to create critical editions of major texts. However, these editions and translations made the texts into something new by superimposing elements of the new European rational mind. The result was to change the whole idea of Language. The original texts were oral and local and therefore accompanied a tradition that provided its own commentary and interpretation. The power and utility of the texts has always been based on the connection between Language and the World. An 'accurate' text was constructed by comparing different editions, finding the most common elements, and coming to conclusions on the basis of 'scientific' experiments. Because the various editions were different, the Europeans deduced that they were all degraded versions of an elusive original. And by extension, all of Indian culture could be seen as a degradation from an original pristine culture, which formed the basis for the unity that became known as Hinduism.

"Now, what is called Hinduism is characterized by a universalist point of view, that mimics this bullshit about all religions ultimately saying the same thing, and therefore focuses on proselytization." Cartouche was becoming more radical by the minute. I was also guilty of being driven by the perennialist thesis that all religions, at a fundamental level express the same truth. Vedanta is always given as the prime example of this. I had fallen for this, as I, too, at least intellectually, located the essence of the Hindu tradition in origins, in the Vedas.

"Still, there are many of us from the West, Cartouche, that reject such cultural arrogance, and have completely embraced Indian culture," I said.

"What I am saying is doubly true for such people. They construct a knowledge of India that is really a reflection of their own culture. For how can they cross the chasm between their Western point of view and another so different? How is it possible for them to examine a language of content by using a language of form? C'mon, Ram Puri Ji! I challenge you with this, for you have been possessed by the ghost of India! You are the site of a competition between the Great Shadow and the ghost of Hari Puri Baba. His and your victory will be to dislodge the Great Shadow from the dominant position of Western culture. In order to do this you must recognize that West and East are equal in their otherness. There is no other way," he said.

How could I be so dumb? I thought to myself, later. Cartouche had gone to the stonecutter's to buy more crystals. He had invited me to come, warning that it might be boring, and I had declined. "How could I doubt my gurus? Even if Hari Puri Baba is inside me, even if what he really wants is to see America."

It wasn't far to walk to Sawai Man Singh Road, and from there I walked to SMS Hospital. I wandered through the Dharamsala guesthouse across the street from the hospital where Amar Puri Baba stayed but decided not to enter the hospital itself. I continued down the large avenue for a while and finally detoured down a smaller street to a small monkey-god Hanuman temple that I used to visit.

I felt terrible. I had let the fact that I was possessed by a baba turn me upside down and had turned my back on everything I had learned. On the basis of a single sentence from an unreliable source, my beloved guru-bhai Kedar Puri Baba, I had been willing to renounce my gurus and my guru tradition. This felt like a sin. Instead of offering my guru refuge, as he had offered me, I had assigned him to the yellowing pages of a book that contained dragons, unicorns, wizards, and other fantastic beings.

I performed my omkars in front of the shiny orange Hanuman, and then I sat in front of him, and with great humility and shame, repeated my guru mantra, counting one hundred and eight repetitions on my rosary.

Hanuman the hero glowed in front of me. His expression betrayed his sense of duty and purpose. Even though one of his feet seemed to be on the ground, he was really flying through the air. I recalled the episode from the story of the *Ramayana*. Lakshman, the brother of Ram, lay slain, along with countless monkey warriors, as Ram attacked the demon Ravan in his kingdom on the island of Lanka, to recover his kidnapped princess. Ram was distraught, and the entire monkey army was disheartened. Everything depended on Hanuman flying to the Himalayas and returning with a rare herb that restores life to the dead before the sun rose on the following day. Needless to say, Hanuman forgot important details and couldn't find the herb. After several misadventures, he mustered his heroic strength, uprooted the entire mountain, and flew back to Lanka holding the mountain in his right hand, so that the monkey physician himself could identify the plant. The image I sat in front of was just that: Hanuman flying back with the mountain. Under his left armpit was a disk. He not only forgot the description of the herb, but he was late. So he also had to kidnap the Sun who, in fact, was his guru, and hide him until he arrived back in Lanka.

I thought of situations of extraordinary strength such as that of the woman who lifted an automobile off her young child. Was Hanuman not pulled by the operation of Sympathy, the Active?

Ram, the Balanced, incarnated to restore order to the Universe, to maintain the Same. This Same, the Active, pulled Hanuman and all the power given to him at birth by all the gods, to the performance of a particular deed. Only a superhero could perform such a thing, and so he succeeded. I remembered Hari Puri Baba telling me that Hanuman was the Lord of Hopeless Causes.

Then it occurred to me that this magical operation of the Active, that drew me into Western discourse, was also drawing me into the sameness of Dattatreya, and the Tradition of Knowledge. It was Hari Puri Baba that was pulling me into him so that I should eventually lose my identity and become him. It is only the operation of antipathy, the Passive, which kept me trying to maintain my individuality. But was it really possible to distinguish myself from this constructed Western Man?

The priest came over and gave me a sweetmeat offering to Hanuman, and applied a tikka of sticky orange sindhur to my third eye. He invited me to have a cup of tea with him in the rear courtyard of the temple, where there was a wrestling ring called an *akhara*. An odd place to wrestle? Hanuman temples often contain wrestling rings and his devotees are often enthusiasts of physical culture. We moved to the back and watched the wrestlers go through their training.

"Besides bathing in the Ganga, how do normal people atone for sins?" I asked the priest. "They make a vow, which could mean a fast, a pilgrimage, or donations to the temple or the poor. There are many ways. It all depends who you are," he said.

"My uncle, who's a strict vegetarian, ran over a frog with his bicycle, and killed it," interjected a young wrestler dripping in sweat and mustard seed oil who decided to take a break.

"Sham Lal Ji, the jeweler on New Road?" asked the priest. The young man nodded.

"Well?" I asked. "What did he do?"

"He wanted to do penance, so he went to the Lakshmi Narayan Temple, and made this known to the head priest there," said the wrestler. "The head priest told him that, being a jeweler, he must have the finest craftsman in Jaipur make a precise copy of the frog in solid gold, and donate it to the temple."

"And . . ." I asked. "Did he do it?"

"Well, sort of," said the young man. "He thought a silver frog would be appropriate, had one of his own junior craftsman make it, and he donated that to the temple."

I thanked the young wrestler for his story, knowing that it was the story of his uncle that had pulled me into the temple.

It was late when I arrived back at Cartouche's room. He had already been back at the hotel for several hours and had stacked a few new boxes of rocks and crystals in the corner.

"What do you know about padukas?" I asked Cartouche.

"Let's see," he replied, "I can tell you that when Ram was banished to the jungle and the king, his father, died, Ram's brother, Bharat, who was put on the throne, found Ram in the jungle and asked him to return to Ayodhya to be king. Ram refused, but gave Bharat his wooden sandals, his padukas, to be placed on the throne in his stead."

"So, who was king, Bharat, or the padukas?" I asked.

"From the people's point of view, it was Bharat, but for Bharat, it was definitely Ram, in the form of his padukas," he said.

"And the padukas at Datt Akhara in Ujjain?" I asked. "Have you heard of those?"

"Who hasn't?" he laughed. "They were the padukas of the Old Pir, that Sandhya Puri Baba kept. My guru used to tell me that they brought the great revival to Datt Akhara under Sandhya Puri Baba. But I'm sure you know much more about it than I do," he said.

"Who was your guru, anyway? Maybe I know him." I inquired.

"You might," he suggested, "after all he was quite close to Hari Puri Baba during Sandhya Puri's days. They all worshipped Sandhya Puri, and thought of him as their guru."

"He was . . . ?" I waited.

"He might not even be around anymore. I haven't seen him since the end of the sixties. He was called Bhairon Baba," he said.

I was stunned and blood rushed to my head. "You couldn't be referring to Bhairon Puri Baba, Cartouche?"

"Yes, that's him, of course," he smiled.

"I can't believe it," I started. "Yes, he's definitely alive. Do you have any idea what kind of a man he is?"

"I believe he is the incarnation of Dattatreya's brother, Durvasa, who was really Shiva, as Dattatreya was really Vishnu. He's an enlightened man, and one of the greatest tantrics in India," he said.

"So why aren't you with him now?" I asked.

"We had sort of a falling out," he said. "It was at the Ujjain Kumbh Mela of 1968. May 1968. You might have been with all the students on the streets of Paris, but I was at the Kumbh. He had offered to make me his formal disciple, and then a sannyasi at the big initiation, and I accepted. But as the day of the first initiation approached, two things happened. The first was that I started to have second thoughts."

"I also had second thoughts," I commented.

"I wasn't sure if I could be a real sadhu! I mean, here I was with a master among yogis and shamans . . . But what if I found out later that it wasn't for me? Would I be able to leave, having made the bond?" Cartouche explained.

"I felt the same thing," I said.

"The second thing that happened had actually been foreshadowed. My Venus was not well aspected for an initiation into sannyas, and I didn't tell Guru Ji," he said.

"How could he not have known?" I asked, "Hari Puri Baba had all that covered."

"Maybe he did, maybe he didn't. But one day, when my guru and your guru were having their usual debate, Hari Puri asked me to search through Ujjain for an English bookstore and bring him a good English dictionary. A strange request, I thought. Having spent half the scorching day in a fruitless search, it must have been 115° in the shade, I found the New Light Bookshop, and that's where I met her."

"Who's *her*?" I asked.

"Marie was from my mother's town near Paris, and she was very beautiful. I fell in love with her on the spot."

"You're kidding, of course."

"Far from it. She had just arrived from France and told me all about the revolution brewing on the streets of Paris. I realized that there was something missing in my life, and it was standing right in front of me."

"So what did you do?"

"What could I do? I backed out of all the initiations, waited until the end of the Kumbh Mela, and took off with my Marie. Bhairon Baba must have known the day I met her. His disappointment grew each day, so that by the time I left, he had already subtracted me from his life. I knew I would never see him again."

"A lot of babas believe he killed Hari Puri Baba with tantra, and he certainly terrorized me since my first day in the akhara," I said.

"I can't believe he killed your baba. He's never killed even a mosquito. I probably really fucked things up for you and every other foreigner . . . Look, they used to debate each other, challenge each other. They would bet, not money, but other things, on winning a particular challenge, but there was nothing fiercer than that."

"Did you have a lot of contact with Hari Puri Baba at that time?" I asked.

"Sure, he'd come over to our dhuni, or we would go to his. Some of the debating involved my discipleship and initiation, and whether or not a foreigner could become a baba. It was clear that I was a problem in the making. Hari Puri even asked me if I had any foreign friends that wanted to be a baba. I didn't, but really wondered just what was going on between them."

"What do you know about Sandhya Puri's padukas?"

"Only that they disappeared from Datt Akhara, and took on the personality of the Holy Grail."

"But surely both Hari Puri and Bhairon Puri had powers, could read the Book of the World, had ways to find them. This is something that I've never figured out about Bhairon Puri. Why hasn't he been able to find them, if he wants them so much?"

"Maybe it's a show, maybe he doesn't really care. He's a guru, not a hero. Hari Puri had even said to me that quest is the cradle of the hero, something I could never forget, it's so, uh, Eliade. And quest is path of the disciple."

19

The Nectar of Immortality

Magic happens anywhere worlds meet. This includes airports, crossroads, the seashore, graveyards, hospitals, and temples, but the places where the Ordinary World meets the Extraordinary World require pilgrimage, either internal or external. The act of making a pilgrimage is that of suspending oneself between worlds. Those locations to which one makes a pilgrimage are called *tirthas*, crossing-over places, and standing on those intersections, one may be in both worlds at the same time. Tirthas mark hidden entrances to the Extraordinary World. They reflect the inner journey onto the external world and reflect the heavens onto the Earth. Those who go on a pilgrimage become like babas for that period.

The main reason for going on pilgrimage is to experience darshan and its blessings, which are made visible by prasad, offerings of flowers, fruit, and sweets given by pilgrims to the deity and then given back to the devotee that seal the bond between humans and God. *Darshan* derives from *drsh*, "to see," and is the Beholding, not "looking," as tourists do, but true Seeing. The prasad—"that which pleases"—is the sign that the deity is pleased and therefore gives blessings. The pilgrim has compassion for the beggars, as he feels the compassion from the deity, so he gives alms as he receives the prasad sacrament. In order that the World benefits from his pilgrimage, the pilgrim brings the blessings (and the prasad) back home.

There are the tirthas of different deities, both local and culture-wide, there are sites where divine events have taken place, and then there are uncountable signatures of nature, but there is one thing all these have in common. They are reflections of the sacred story that is played out in the stars. A gateway stands in that hinge between the reflections.

Pilgrimage is also story: each pilgrim is a hero and every hero has a quest. In the Extraordinary World, acceptance means connecting with the stars and reflecting the story told there onto the surface of the Earth. It means achieving a kind of immortality by living on in story when the body is no longer here.

Amar Puri Baba neither scolded me nor even seemed to remember my little freak-out, when I returned to him several months later. He hardly even acknowledged that I had been away. When the old Pir of Datt Akhara finally left his body at the age of one hundred and eighteen, a conclave of the akhara's senior most babas elected Amar Puri to be the new Pir just in time to preside over and host the Ujjain Kumbh Mela of 1979. This was a great victory for our family lineage, and Amar Puri was now called a *siddha,* "an accomplished one," by all the babas. We all moved to Ujjain, were assigning specific sacred duties, and started preparing for the great Kumbh. But, a month before the mela was to begin, he suddenly died, leaving behind utter chaos.

Now that my two main gurus were dead, my priorities began to change. I spent the next few years based in Kashi at the invitation from Kapil Puri Baba, who became my patron, and eventually another of my gurus through initiation. But the younger generation of babas was coming into its own, and being very much part of this generation, I made pilgrimages to the four corners of India with my peers.

I celebrated a twelve-year reunion with my fellow initiates at the Allahabad Kumbh Mela of 1983, which was also the cycle of Jupiter. It amazed me that twelve years had already passed since I became a baba. I was reminded by Bam Baba, who kept appearing in my life, that I still hadn't made a pilgrimage to the source of the Ganga, high in the Himalayas.

"The path to the thousand-petaled lotus lies to the north," said Bam Baba, referring to the spinning energy center behind my eyebrows, the *ajna* chakra, command central, which corresponds to the confluence of the rivers, and the path leading to the top of my head, which corresponds to the source of the Ganga. "The world moves steadily forward, but we walk in the opposite direction," said the big baba, "toward the source."

Hardwar, some seven hundred miles northwest of Allahabad, is a bustling pilgrim center nestled in the foothills of the Himalayas, where the Ganga leaves the mountains and enters the expansive plains of north India. The town lies on the right bank of the Ganga as she flows south. Look north and see the giant pillars that are the Shivalik Hills, entrance to the Land of the Gods: look south and see the plains, the hot, dusty world of mortals. Hardwar is a gateway. *Dwar* means door. It even sounds like the English word. That door was not an accident of nature but a link between the worlds. Har-dwar is the gateway of the great god, Shiva, also called Har or Hara.

"Hara Hara Mahadev!"
Hail to the Great God Shiva,
Whose name is Hara!

Some call the town, Haridwar, the gateway of the sustaining god, Vishnu, also known as Hari, while others call it Gangadwar, the gateway of the Ganga, or even Brahmadwar, the gateway of the creator god, Brahma. But the most ancient name of Hardwar is Mayadwar, the door of illusion.

The gateway wasn't always there; neither was the Ganga. The Shivalik Hills stood as a proud wall sealing off the Land of the Gods until they were ripped apart by the ferocious assault of the fertile river goddess on its ramparts, so that she could carry her fecundity down to the north Indian plains and the human race.

I left Allahabad with Bir Giri Baba, who became like a brother on a pilgrimage to the Source, but we made it only as far as Hardwar, where I became sidetracked by the lure of owning my own ashram. We camped for a couple months on an island in the Ganga, the ancient meditation grounds for yogis called the *tapu,* "where austerities are performed," while we waited for the snows to melt on our path to the Source. One day, our host, an old baba who had been sitting there at his dhuni for twenty-five years, told me that a small plot of land with an old house, right on the bank of the Ganga, was for sale. He suggested that if I could raise the money, about ninety thousand rupees (about ten thousand dollars at the time) I should buy it.

I could have sworn that I recognized the land from dreams I had of Hari Puri. I thought I even heard his voice inside of me chanting "Buy it, buy it!" But how could I ever get that much cash. Bir Giri shook his head. "Don't look at *me,*" he said.

Evidently the news had reached Kapil Puri Baba, who in turn put the word out to all the devotees and babas of our family lineage, for within two weeks, donations started pouring in until we had our requisite sum.

I named our new refuge, on the northern bank of the Ganga a

few hundred feet downstream from Hardwar's cremation ground, Hari Puri Ashram.

By the time of the Hardwar Kumbh of 1986, my diaries had grown to more than a thousand pages, and I had also collected numerous other texts, despite Hari Puri's insistence that the written word would be of limited use. I began organizing my notes, referencing Sanskrit texts, and writing about the secret oral teachings I had received.

During the Kumbh, our kitchen fed a hundred mouths a day in addition to non-stop chai. Visitors arrived from all over India bringing donations and gifts for the ashram, and we started making plans to expand, to build more rooms and halls, a *ghat* of broad steps down to the river, and statues of Hari Puri Baba (I had promised him) and Amar Puri Baba.

When the mela ended, several groups of babas left for a pilgrimage to Gangotri-Gaumukh, as it is especially auspicious to go after a Hardwar Kumbh Mela. I turned down many invitations to join them on the trek to the source of the Ganga, because of my responsibilities at the ashram, as well as my self-appointed task to record the knowledge of an oral tradition.

And then one day I became ill. I thought it must have been the hot milk Nikku served me before bed. Perhaps it was spoiled. At that time we had not yet built toilets, so we would use the jungle bordering the ashram. As I got weaker by the day, I was repeatedly making trips into the jungle, and watching the dead burn in the adjacent cremation grounds. I had internal bleeding and none of the herbs that a baba administered to me had any effect.

One day I had trouble standing, and I realized that I might be dying. If I didn't make it to a good hospital fast, I would soon join my gurus. A devotee drove me to a friend in Delhi, but before I could even greet him, I passed out, and regained consciousness days later at a modern hospital. The doctors couldn't determine what was wrong with me, so they called it a viral fever, an all-encompassing term for mystery diarrhea. However, I had been hemorrhaging, and I started to suspect foul play.

What doesn't kill you makes you stronger, and within a couple of weeks, I had regained my strength, and returned to Hardwar. I was shocked when I arrived at the bustling ashram and found it not only completely deserted but also stripped bare. The doors were wide open, not a soul in sight, and not so much as a piece of cloth on the ground. It had been ransacked.

"Nikku Baba did it," said Madan Lal, one of our devotees, as I stood there devastated. "He threw everything into the Ganga."

"And nobody did anything to stop him?" I asked incredulously.

"He was all alone. Bir Giri Baba went to Kashi and left him in charge, and he shooed everyone away," said Madan Lal.

"Everything?" I asked.

"Maybe not, " he said, but I didn't believe him. "You had better find him quickly, if you want to try to get anything back. He's gone to Gangotri-Gaumukh."

I felt as though I had died, and, in fact, part of me had done so. My shadow self who, despite all the warnings, had recorded fragments of knowledge for years and who lived in the pages of my diaries, had met a violent end. After a brief mourning period for this fellow, I read the writing on the wall, and it said that it was time to make good on my pledge to reach The Source. I realized that I had brought the desecration upon myself by being sidetracked by the very possessions that were now gone. There was nothing to be gained by tracking down Nikku Baba, as he was only a puppet of my fate. Perhaps he was actually doing me a favor by eliminating my physical as well as mental baggage, freeing me to complete my pilgrimage.

I caught an early morning bus that put me in Gangotri by night-fall, the end of the motorable road. I spent the night by the dhuni of a baba whose name I never learned, and set off walking to the source before dawn. Climbing thirteen miles from nine to eleven thousand feet, I reached the source by late morning.

Gaumukh is the meeting place of the world of ice, the primordial Gangotri Glacier, and the world of water, the River Ganga. Frozen eternity becomes dynamic change as water oozes out and huge blocks thunder into the Ganga's virgin pool. Always retreating into her father Himalaya's lair, the twenty-thousand-foot peak also named Gangotri, the source of the Ganga had moved back almost a mile since my initiation there as a baba twelve years before.

I walked above the Ganga, which flows through a canyon carved out over millions of years by the giant razor blade of a glacier. The rocky trail led me through small forests of firs and past streams flowing down the mountain. And looming above me was the great Himalayan range and eventually the majestic peak Shivling (Shiva's phallus). After I passed through the last trees, a grove of silver birch, frequented by yogis over the millennia, I climbed the final couple of miles over rocks and boulders. The contrast between a world wrapped in ignorance and the universe of beauty and sanctity was astounding.

Overlooking Gaumukh there was a tent, where I would probably find everyone including Nikku Baba, but before entering, I decided to take a dip in the source of the Ganga, as this is the first duty of a pilgrim. Normally Gaumukh is a flat ice face. The glacier ends, the river begins, and that is that. On this occasion Gaumukh looked like an ice cave, but once I saw her up close, she appeared to be a temple open to the sky. Although I am not brave, I was overcome with the desire to penetrate the sanctuary to its depths.

Inside, everything was frozen. When the sun's rays hit the ice palace, I was knocked to my knees. The Goddess revealed herself as splintered beams of multicolored light refracting off her crystalline body, shimmering, appearing, and then changing, blushing pinks turning to aquamarine blues. This was the darshan.

Carrying my empty kamandal in my right hand, I pushed away the sharp sheets of ice as I waded in up to my thighs. My legs burned in the glacial water. When I reached what they call the Seat of the Midwife in the middle of the nascent stream, I rinsed my mouth and dunked three times. My heart stopped, my lungs shrieked, and I was suspended in time. Then came a rush of heat, a fire blazed within me, burning the skin all over my body. I filled my kamandal and returned to the shore. My head was cold but my skin had tightened and the rest of me was on fire. I sat on the glacier in my loincloth, lit some incense, and tossed a red flower I had picked on the path into the waters. I said mantras, expressed my gratitude for the intensity of the darshan, and beseeched the Mother of Waters to bless the world with peace. I went on to request that if that wasn't possible, then to bless a few people whose names I recited. An old pilgrim watched me with amazement. I started to shiver as the clouds covered the sun and quickly put on my clothes and covered myself in a wool shawl.

"Baba Ji," said the old pilgrim as he approached, "I feel so ashamed. I've come all the way from Calcutta, and made it up here to the Ganga's source, yet I am afraid to have my sacred bath. It's too cold. I cannot do what you did."

"But you can!" I told him. "Take off your shoes and socks. Wash your feet, then your hands and face, rinse your mouth, and throw a couple of drops over your head. That will complete your holy bath, sir."

"You mean, I don't have to immerse myself?" he asked.

"No," I said, "this is the tradition."

He followed my instructions and offered me his sincere thanks for my help. The clouds now turned black, and I made a dash for the tent as it began to pour. I was drenched by the time I arrived at the large green army tent, whose entrance was piled high with shoes. Inside the smoky tent, which was crowded with boisterous babas, a celebration seemed to be taking place.

Even though several babas greeted me by name, I didn't recognize anyone. This wasn't unusual: I had become something of a celebrity, being the rare foreign sadhu. "We heard Nikku Baba had poisoned you," said one. "We heard you were in the hospital," said another. I explained that I hadn't been poisoned but had been ill, and was now fully recovered. No one had seen Nikku, however.

I threaded my way to the far end and after paying my respects to the dhuni, sat down next to the fire. There was a lone baba, covered in a blanket, sitting on the raised platform behind the dhuni, with his back to everyone.

"So you have finally come to see me," said the baba. I couldn't immediately place the voice but it sounded oddly familiar. I gasped when he turned around to face me. It was Bhairon Puri Baba.

I panicked. I had stumbled into the tiger's lair, having been properly washed and sanctified for his supper. This time there would be no escape. There were no Hari Puri Babas, Amar Puri Babas, or Kapil Puri Babas. Only Bhairon Puri and me.

The wind continued hitting the tent with such force, that despite the hundred-pound stones that held down the canvas, I thought we would fly away. Thunder rolled down from the Himalayan peaks and reverberated through the canyons below.

I fumbled through my bag-of-wishes for a ten-rupee note and a one-rupee coin that I put under his foot, which I touched with my forehead. In times of doubt, show maximum respect.

"Well, what do you want?" he asked.

"I want to know the truth," I said meekly.

"Yes, the truth—such an elusive thing. It hides from prying eyes," he said. "And what are you prepared to pay for it?"

I felt very threatened and clasped my hands in front of my face.

"Okay, fair enough, I think you're ready. . . ." he said, smoothing his long white beard and looking me squarely in the eyes. "It was a bet, and he won."

"What?" I asked. "I don't believe you."

"You may believe what you wish," Bhairon Puri replied.

"So you *killed* him?" I asked bravely.

Bhairon Puri grunted. "Ram, Ram, Ram! What do you know, child," he said. "He was my brother, as Cartouche is yours. Do you think I don't miss him? He was the finest baba I ever knew and nobody had greater love than I for Hari Puri Baba."

I was confused, and Bhairon Puri read this on my face.

"Ah, you think I don't know about your meetings with Cartouche Baba? Hari Puri believed a foreigner could never become a baba. I disagreed and challenged him, saying that becoming a baba had nothing to do with one's birthplace. To prove my case, I started training Cartouche, but when Cartouche walked out of the Ujjain Kumbh Mela, I conceded defeat to your guru. But he wasn't satisfied. He claimed that I hadn't tried hard enough. He was not willing to accept an incomplete victory. "I must help you to correct my arrogance, I will prove my own dogma wrong," he said.

"You see, your guru used to say that the truth shall set you free. And he had a power of intellect that was unmatched by anyone, only, that is, by the truth. So he decided to make a Sacrifice of Knowledge reflecting God's covenant that humans may have a path and a way to know him. He decided to enter you, for that is the way that babas are made, but had to give up his body to do so. I tried everything I could do to stop him, but he wouldn't listen to reason. Our wager was Dattatreya's padukas . . ."

Back to page one, just as I thought I had it all figured out.

"This is the way it happens. When Baba likes you, he goes inside, and then they call *you* 'Baba.' In the same way Baba went into our Hari Puri," he said.

Bhairon Puri Baba captured me with his words. I knew what he meant now, and as I studied his face, I saw first Hari Puri Baba, then Amar Puri Baba, and then something else. It suddenly became very clear to me: Baba is not a man.

"Baba does the choosing, and you, fortunately, have not had to undertake your quest alone. Your gurus, elders, and heroes from the beginning of time have gone before you marking the path. And now you have come to the source. I see your kamandal is full. Drink from it, and share it with me. Cool, refreshing liquid. Drink deeply!"

And I did. The Nectar of Immortality spilled onto Time, erasing mortality forever. The water from the source of the Ganga awakened Hari Puri Baba from his sleep, and then his guru, Sandhya Puri Baba, and the one hundred thousand and eight babas whose bodies had already carried knowledge through the barrier of death. And all of them entered my being.

Bhairon Puri chanted quietly:

> *Searching the wide world,*
> *I have come to the core of my own being;*
> *All alone, I am with everyone.*

The nectar was intoxicating and soon carried me off into a deep sleep. When I awoke at dawn, Bhairon Puri Baba had gone, as had most of the other babas. I had a second bath in the Ganga, and then I also departed for the world below.

Just before I reached Bhojbasa, I turned around and saw a young baba running down the last mountain pass. When he caught up with me, he handed me a package. "Baba Ji told me to give this to you, but I forgot," he explained. "He said you might need them."

The wooden sandals inside the package were way too small for me to wear on my Western feet, but I took them for a sign that the ancient path of knowledge does indeed exist. I put them into my bag-of-wishes for safekeeping and continued on my way to my ashram in Hardwar, that door between the world of gods and the world of mortals.

Afterword

I've always had an odd sense of timing. On September 10, 2001, I e-mailed a couple chapters and an outline for *BABA* [title of the original edition] off to the States from my home high in the Himalayan foothills. I learned patience in India, but when I hadn't heard a word for three months, I sent another e-mail and got the following response, "Everyone's still watching television."

I completed the original manuscript of *BABA* on the last possible day on which I could still drive my jeep 1,200 kilometers to Ujjain, pick up my guru-bhais, Paramanand Puri Ji (made Pir of Datt Akhara the following year) and Sundar Puri Ji, and then another 600 kilometers to the Kumbh Mela at Nasik, before they barricaded the road.

At the Kumbh, many of the Naga Babas came to know about the manuscript, and put their marks, signs, and blessings on the cover. The high priests from the Mahakal (Father Time) Temple in Ujjain visited us during that time, and agreed to offer the work to Mahakal Himself (Shiva). At the end of the Mela, I gave my only copy of *BABA* to Vijay Guru, the Head Priest, who took the volume back to Ujjain, and made the offering in an elaborate ceremony. "It's *His*, now," he explained to me later when he returned the manuscript.

A week later, Random House offered to buy the book.

I was very privileged to work with Toinette Lippe as my editor on the original edition of *BABA*. It could only be blessings manifest to work with a brilliant woman who during her forty some years as an editor with three of the largest publishing houses in the world, edited many of the classic books on spirituality, India, and Eastern Religions—and was proficient in Sanskrit.

Not that it was always a pleasant experience, far from it, after all she was the scissors lady looking at your baby, but Kapil Puri Ji used to say, "It's only by *sangharsh,* "friction," and "struggle," that gold is purified from its ore."

A writer friend of mine told me that it is *always* a struggle, but considers it the "good fight."

We were opposites. In getting to know each other, I named James Joyce and Salman Rushdie as my favorite authors. "Oh, I so dislike both of them!" she replied. I told her what turns me on in literature was the *sound* of the words, she, however, cherished the *meanings* of the words. It felt to me at the time that magic and science were meeting head to head.

And I don't mean the details of phrasing a sentence or cutting out a paragraph. Here is where it becomes relevant to you, the reader.

Our first major issue was the genre of *BABA*—I told her that my manuscript was a work of fiction.

"You mean it *didn't happen?*" she gasped in horror, Random House having sent me my first check.

"Of course it all happened," I had to smile, "and much more that I don't dare write for risk of losing believability."

The difference between fiction and non-fiction has nothing to do with truth, but with the style of storytelling; fiction uses analogy, non-fiction, linear reasoning. There are countless works of non-fiction having not a grain of truth, but good reasoning and works of fiction that contain some of the highest truths, but little linear reasoning. Mythology is fiction, writing about mythology is non-fiction.

But, what about the Bible? It's categorized as non-fiction.

Don't get me started. I can only question, "Who does the categorizing?"

I had nothing to sell (besides the book), no thesis, no argument to make, nothing to convince people of, and no modern history to write.

> *I no longer want to be an outsider, an exploiter,*
> *a pillager of knowledge.*

I couldn't be anyone's or any ideology's agent, I could only represent myself, the subject.

So my primary purpose of writing *BABA* was to entertain you; to take my readers on a trip in the extraordinary world, and if that excursion is compelling enough, if I may hold my reader's consciousness for a rubber moment, then he or she may be curious to look around at that world and explore it deeper with all its implications.

In the five years that have passed since the first edition of *BABA* in English, and subsequent editions in Russian, German, and Serbian, I've met many of my readers around the world, giving talks and workshops. But the one question that my audiences have been too polite to ask me, but begs asking is "What the hell does living in a cave naked in a land far away with a bunch of eccentric renunciates, have to do with my life as a mother of three in New Jersey, or a computer techie in Latvia, or an air-force pilot in Belgrade?"

So I ask it for them, because until this question is asked, we have no ground to stand on and nowhere to go.

Nothing to buy into here. If you should tell me that, having read the book, you now want to become a Naga Baba, I'd tell you, "Forget it." What for?

And there is no "message." In the thirties, Samuel Goldwyn famously told his script writers, "If you want to send a message, call Western Union." Now you can send an e-mail.

But from the time of man's first Ritual, and through it's child, Theater and it's companion, Storytelling, if something is compelling enough, entertaining enough, to grab your consciousness, as our action heroes do in our films and newspapers, then in that space where two worlds meet, magic can happen, knowledge and prosperity obtained.

Storytelling is a boat transporting knowledge across the Ocean of Story. The sky, witnessing and reflecting the world, has a nightly series that has been playing forever.

For like the night sky, Storytelling is an enigmatic mirror, reflecting not the Ordinary World, but an Analogue World. Looking at yourself as this reflection, you see the ultimate subject, the creator of all you see, hear, feel, and think, and as such, the possessor of royal blood. That land in your background is holy land, those concrete phalli mark hidden things (often wealth), the rivers are great goddesses, the mountains ancient kings, and then, of course, there are those places where worlds meet.

My gurus have all left their bodies; they died, one by one. Arjun Puri Ji, being the oldest, was the last to leave. Bir Giri Ji is also gone. At one point, it seemed like a mass exodus. Strangely enough, of all the babas I named and wrote about, only I remain.

Tradition survives the deaths of its masters. The responsibility for this survival falls onto the shoulders of the disciple, who, like me, wanted only to explore the magic of the extraordinary world and honor those beings that inhabit it.

The disciple feels the gravity of the sky—slowly being pulled into the stars and their mythology, as he or she realizes the gravity of the situation—the mechanism of tradition is that the disciple indeed shall become the guru. There is no other way.

Storytelling is a boat crossing time with a payload of knowledge as colossal as the ocean of story itself. And so, a songbook passed into my pocket.

Glossary

acharya: The akara's supreme spiritual authority.

akhara: Order of the Sannyasi tradition.

amrit: Divine nectar of eternal life, literally "no-death."

asan: Seat or sitting pad also posture and sitting posture.

baba: Guru and teacher of the Sannyasi tradition.

barat: Entourage.

bhajan: Hymns sung to the Gods and Goddesses.

bhandara: A feast among Sannyasis and laymen.

chela: Disciple. Also called *shishya*.

chillam: A cylindrical clay pipe, which is wider at the top. Cannabis or Charas mixed with cigarette tobacco is smoked in it.

chimpta: Iron tongs used to operate the sacred fire of the Dhuni.

dakshina: A gift of money to honor a baba, teacher, or priest.

dargah: The tomb of a Sufi holy person.

darshan: Derived from the Sanskrit root *drsh* or "to see," the word means literally "revelation." It is used when a person experiences the majesty of a great personality, a God, or a wonder of nature.

Dattatreya: The three-headed Lord of the Yogis, shamans, tantrics, and alchemists; the heads are those of Brahma, Vishnu, and Shiva.

devalok: The divine world of the Gods.

dhoti: A large thin cloth that men wear wrapped around their hips as a skirt.

dhuni: The fire pit, or seat of the sacred fire.

Extraordinary World: In the upper case meaning the reality beyond, above or even outside daily rationality, the world opposed to the ordinary where natural laws are no longer valid or have been suspended or changed.

Ganga Snan: A sacred bath in the holy river Ganga.

ganja: Marijuana.

ghats: Stone steps leading down to a river.

gotra: Indian clan.

guru: Spiritual teacher.

guru bhai: Spiritual brother who is a student of the same guru.

janeu: The string of the "Twice-Born," that Brahmins wear over their left shoulder, but babas use to thread the rudraksha seed and wear around their necks.

japa: The daily repetition of a mantra over several days, and sometimes, even years.

jholi: The small, richly decorated shoulder bag of a sadhu that he has always with him, and contains everything he needs.

kamandal: A water jug with a wide handle, one of the few possessions of a Sannyasi. It holds water but also Amrit, the sacred nectar of eternal life.

katori: A small bowl made mostly out of steel or copper.

kotwali: Baba cop.

Kumbh Mela: The largest festival in the world where sacrifices are tendered, and Sannyasis of the baba tradition are inducted.

Kundalini: Name of a Goddess of Knowledge, a consort of Shiva, seen as a serpent wrapped three and a half times around the Shiva Ling at the base of the spine where a sitting person connects with the Earth. Her analogic rise to the top of the head reflects the process of knowledge and illumination as the objective world merges with the subjective.

kurta: An Indian-style collarless shirt.

lingoti: Loincloth.

mantra: Sacred syllables used for invocation.

Om: The most significant of mantras containing within it all other mantras.

omkar: Deference due to a Guru, with particular prostrations, touching the feet, and the recitation of mantras.

padukas: The sandals of the God Dattatreya who left them on the Earth to show his presence; a sign of discipleship and knowledge.

pandit: A religious teacher-priest.

parcha: A receipt.

pir: Usually the title of a Muslim Sufi leader, but it is also the title of the abbot of Datt Akhara in Ujjain.

pranayam: The control and regulation of breath.

prasad: A sacrificial offering in the form of flowers, fruit, and sweets by pilgrims to the divinities that are returned after the ritual to the Faithful.

puja: Ritual.

rishi(s): The ancestors of mankind, the composers/authors of the sacred Vedas, and the source and the blood of the Indian people.

rudraksha: Grown out of a teardrop of Shiva when he saw the state of mankind. The students of a guru would present him with the seeds as the symbol of the student body and manifest the link between mankind and the God Shiva.

sadhana: Spiritual work.

sadhu: A yogi shaman and ascetic who has renounced the world.

sangam: A sacred confluence—the divine meeting of rivers.

sannyas: The path of renunciation for which man must be consecrated.

sannyasi: An initiate into the order of renunciates founded by Adi Shankaracharya 2,500 years ago.

seva: Service to a guru or a cause.

siddha: Someone who is successful in the "Extraordinary World" and possesses extra-normal powers called *siddhis*.

siddhi: Supernormal powers and abilities that a yogi or sannyasi acquires.

Shiva: One of the trinity of the Indian Gods, accompanying Brahma, who creates the universe, and Vishnu, who maintains it. Shiva, often thought of as the Destroyer, is more accurately described as "withdrawing" the universe to its original source, Pure Subjective Consciousness, which he personifies. Because of his withdrawing nature, he is thought of as the original baba, the Outsider, and called *Mahadev,* Supreme among the Gods.

sutra: A highly compressed and esoteric style of Sanskrit Language that conveys a great body of knowledge in very few syllables.

tapas: Austerities.

tapasvi: One who practices austerities.

tirth: A holy place; a place of "crossing over," where the worlds meet each; Taken from the Sanskrit root *tr,* which is in Latin *trans* and means crossing.

vibhuti: The ashes of the sacred fire, used for blessings, protection, medicine, alchemy, and magic.

Vidyar Sanskar: The ritual of becoming a sannyasi; the sacrament of entry into the "Extraordinary World" (see entry above), when the aspirant performs his own ritual cremation and cuts all ties to his past.

yatra: Pilgrimage.